"'Not everybody talking at Tony Beckett. Turning to the Scriptures for understanding of this much-used but little-practiced word, Dr. Beckett reminds us that true worship cannot be reduced to a 'weekend activity.' Rather, it is a response to God that should consume all our hours and characterize every dimension of our lives. This insightful and practical book calls us to become true worshipers, offering up the kind of worship that He alone deserves."

Nancy Leigh DeMoss
Author, conference and radio speaker

"*Real Life, Real Worship* is really challenging and really fresh. Tony Beckett has written a book on worship that incorporates the thinking of some of God's choicest, worshipful saints. Most important, it draws upon the worship Book and points us to the One we worship."

Paul Dixon
President
Cedarville University

"Worship, which is the highest occupation of a man before his God, has fallen on hard times. With that in mind, I am delighted to recommend *Real Life, Real Worship,* which hits at the very heart of the real meaning of worship.

"Tony Beckett does not emphasize music or emotions but rather the heart-centered adoration of our great God in every step of life, not just the fleeting experience of one hour on Sunday morning."

Joe Jordan
Executive Director
Word of Life Fellowship

"My friend Tony Beckett reminds me that although worship is often the most divisive aspect of church life, it ought to be the most decisive—yielding all we are to who the Lord is. In fact, I'm giving copies of *Real Life, Real Worship* to those leading worship in our church."

Dr. Gene A. Getz
Senior Pastor
Fellowship Bible Church North

REAL LIFE
REAL WORSHIP

Developing the Heart that God Desires

TONY BECKETT

Tony Beckett
2 Cor 12:9

BACK TO THE BIBLE
Publishing

BACK TO THE BIBLE PUBLISHING
P. O. Box 82808
Lincoln, Nebraska 68501

Editor: Anne Severance
Assistant editor: Rachel Derowitsch
Cover design: Laura Poe
Cover photos: Mel Curtis/PhotoDisc
Interior design: Robert Greuter and Associates
Art and editorial direction: Kim Johnson

Additional copies of this book are available from Back to the Bible Publishing. You may order by calling 1-800-759-2425 or through our Web site at www.resources.backtothebible.org.

1 2 3 4 5 6 7 8 9 10 – 06 05 04 03 02 01

ISBN 0-8474-6518-7

Printed in the USA

To Joan
my best friend, my lover, my helpmeet.

To the daughters God has given us —
Katie, Bekah, and Lauren.

And to Mark . . .
May the life he and Bekah establish together
be as blessed and fulfilling
as the one I share with my wife.

ACKNOWLEDGMENTS

On the road traveled by those who worship the true God there will be fellow pilgrims, others who desire more than an event, who seek the fullness of a life lived in response to God. These kindred spirits do more than merely accompany us along the path—they encourage, teach, correct, enlist, and join us in bringing praise to God. I am abundantly grateful for the multitude of traveling companions whom I have encountered in churches around the world and in books authored by people with varying perspectives.

I am thankful for other worship seekers and for those who have ministered to my soul through their teaching, music, and example. Among those who stand out are the people of Heritage Baptist Church, whom I served as pastor. I still delight in the remembrance of sitting next to Brian Maxwell on the front row—side by side, pastor and worship leader—as the worship service unfolded. I am thankful for him and others who have joined in proclaiming, "Worthy is the Lamb!"

TABLE OF CONTENTS

FOREWORD

In recent years, God has been calling His people back to total living instead of merely occasional doing, and those who have heeded the call have found new freedom, joy, and power in the Christian walk.

For example, we've learned that we shouldn't just do witnessing—we are witnesses, twenty-four hours a day. "Lifestyle evangelism" is replacing toggle-switch evangelism, the kind that's turned on and off as the occasion requires. We're also learning that living is giving, and the "giving-living" goes far beyond putting contributions in the offering plate or sending checks in the mail. We live to give, not just of our substance but also of ourselves, and our giving enriches our living.

This book calls us to a life of total worship, not just the once-a-week kind that eases our conscience but doesn't change our lives. When living means the constant worship of God, we find that our lives are expanding and we're enriching the stated times of corporate worship when we meet with God's people. Vance Havner used to say that the average church worship service starts at eleven o'clock sharp and ends at twelve o'clock dull. But that wouldn't happen if we were worshiping God all day long, all week long, and not just on Sundays.

Tony Beckett has discerningly examined recent trends in worship and explained why the church is frantically grasping at substitutes instead of laying hold of the real experience of worship that can be ours. Styles of worship change from time to time and from place to place, but the spiritual essence of true worship remains the same and should govern our lives at all times and in all places.

With courage and candor—and an occasional chuckle—the author leads us down a biblical path that brings us face-to-face with the inescapable question: "Will I make worship the heart of my life or just a part of my life?"

Imagine what would happen to our lives, homes, and churches if all of us made the right decision!

Warren W. Wiersbe

INTRODUCTION

In the dynamics of church life today, a high priority is placed on worship. According to a study conducted by the Barna organization, an overwhelming majority of Christians desire a consistently positive worship experience: "If the Christian Church is called to help people know, love and serve God through six foundational faith practices — worship, evangelism, discipleship, fellowship, stewardship and compassionate service — then the aspect that the greatest number of churchgoers embrace is worship."[1]

Yet most Christians do not sense the presence of God during the services they attend — men much less often than women. Thus disappointed week after week, they are frustrated and confused by their inability to connect with God on a deeper level.

Unfortunately, the search for meaningful worship too often heads in the direction of improved technology, or imitating what seems to work elsewhere, or trying some new worship technique or tip from the experts. The best approach, however — though admittedly more difficult — is one of inner change. A heart change.

Less than half of all worshipers do anything to prepare themselves for times of corporate worship. Many, if not most, reserve worship as a special weekend activity and find themselves struggling to clear their minds to focus on God. Walking into the door of a church may be like throwing an electrical switch to the "on" position, but true worship cannot be turned off and on at will like the ceiling light in your kitchen.

To stand before the Lord in a time of worship, to see the faces of others who are connecting with God, to hear singing that is truly from the heart — to desire all of that but not experience it for yourself is like an incomplete sentence. You wait for the next phrase, but it doesn't come. Soon you're "lip-synching" — you know when to stand, when to sing, when to sit, when to bow your head . . . and when to leave. What you may not have learned is how to worship.

For corporate worship to be most meaningful, the Christ-follower must embrace a worship lifestyle that is far more comprehensive than the few times spent together in church. The prophet Jonah, in spite of his disobedience, identified himself as a worshiper: "I am a Hebrew and I worship the LORD, the God of heaven, who made the sea and the land" (Jonah 1:9). His self-description was not a statement of church attendance but of a manner of life.

For many others, worship is like a shiny new musical instrument that is kept in a case, opened only at church in the presence of others. The would-be worshiper may desire to use that instrument to play beautiful music, but without practice during the week, the result may be disastrous. The notes are more noise than music, discordant, off-key. So the instrument is put back into the case.

Take worship out of that imaginary case and look it over. Nowhere does it bear the inscription "For Church Use Only." Worship is more, much more than that.

Yes, we gather together as the people of God to praise His name in song, in prayer, in tithes and offerings, and in proclamation of the Word. Surprisingly, that is the narrow view of worship. The broad view is whole-life worship, in which hearts are prepared for corporate praise through daily interaction with God. Whole-life worship is not something we take out of the case occasionally, but the box into which we place everything we are, everything we have, and everything we hope to become. Into this box go all of our days, all of our activities, all of our thoughts and dreams. It is "the necessary foundation for all our praise and adoration, both privately and corporately," writes Jerry Bridges in his book *I Exalt You, O God.*[2] It is the life of worship, one in which worship is made real and relevant, that will bring the most fulfillment.

"To attempt to worship God in only the narrow sense of praising Him without also seeking to worship Him in our whole way of life is hypocrisy. Jesus rebuked the Pharisees because they were going through outward motions of worship, but their hearts were not committed to God. 'You hypocrites!' he said. 'Isaiah was right when he prophesied about you: "These people honor me with their lips, but their hearts are far from me. They worship me in vain; their teaching are but rules taught by men"' (Matt. 15:7-9)."[3]

They understood worship in the specific, narrow sense but failed to worship in the broad sense. Their failure was so great that none of their worship was acceptable to God.

So, it's Sunday. The bulletin in your hand says, "Welcome to our worship service." During the next hour or so, there will be prayer, praise, offerings, proclamation, and invitation—all recognized elements of modern-day worship. But will there be true communion with God, heart-to-heart?

What is needed is real life, real worship—intertwined and lived out so that they become synonymous. When to live is to worship the God who gave us life, then worship will be real—every day.

CHAPTER 1

REAL LIFE, REAL WORSHIP

Job 1

"Your thoughts of God are too human."
—Martin Luther, speaking to Erasmus

It's early morning. The mind is still in a sleep-induced fog and the bleary eyes are struggling to focus. But the feet still work, moving in a shuffle-step toward the kitchen. You find your way to the table, cup of coffee in hand in hopes of jump-starting your brain with a jolt of caffeine.

You have strayed long enough from the path that leads from the bedroom to the kitchen to retrieve the newspaper from the front porch. Except today the paperboy's aim was off, and you had to fish it out of the hydrangea bushes.

Usually you take time only to scan the front page, sorting through the articles until you spot some item of interest. This day, however, will be different.

There is nothing subtle about the headline. Blasted into a heightened state of awareness, your brain processes the startling news: "Local Business Bankrupt." At closing time yesterday, management locked the doors and sent out a press release. All remaining assets of the bankrupt business will be turned over to a receiver, although almost everything has been squandered, including the retirement funds.

You set aside the cup of coffee. No need now for caffeine. You're wide awake. Those people in the picture accompanying the news report are your coworkers. In spite of having worked together for years, nobody had a clue that there were financial difficulties. Even recent meetings with the human resources director about the possibility of early retirement had done nothing to give you the slightest concern about the security of your investments. But now, everything has changed. You've been robbed!

Would you, at that moment, feel inclined to worship God?

◆

At the end of a long day, you snuggle into the comfort of your own bed—the familiar pillow, the smell of clean sheets, the well-earned rest that is soon to follow. The household has settled down for the night, and your kids know to come in quietly from the ball game. They're good kids and you trust them not to violate curfew, so no need to wait up until they get home.

Then . . . sometime in the middle of the night, the telephone rings. A quick glance at the clock reveals the time: 2:00 A.M. This can't be good news. Maybe it's a wrong number.

You fumble for the receiver, mumbling a muted "hello." The voice on the other end of the line speaks in subdued tones. A police officer is calling from the hospital to report an accident. A vehicle with four occupants has collided with an oncoming SUV. The driver and all three passengers are dead. Your children were in that car!

A call in the night . . . but a call to worship?

◆

In the doctor's office, you await the results of tests. You can read the truth in the doctor's grim expression before he says a word. You didn't need a physician to tell you that something was wrong, but you were hoping it would be something minor. Not . . . this. *Give me something to celebrate, God, and I will worship—but I can't worship You from the grave!*

◆

When you think about worship, what comes to mind as the catalyst for praise? Is it a well-appointed church sanctuary, where the people are gathered, instruments playing, the choir singing familiar songs and anthems? Or is it a more solitary setting, with soft, meditative music in the background as you reflect, pray, and read God's Word, uninterrupted by the thoughts and prayers of others around you?

What stirs you to worship? Surely not the scenarios we have pictured here. We tend to associate worship with sanctuaries and quiet places, music and joyful celebration. Not financial disasters, theft, illness, and death. Yet it really is "all of the above." The times of singing and the times of silence, even the news we never wanted to hear—all prompt us to praise God because real worship takes place in real life.

The Agony and the Ecstasy (vv. 13–22)

Job knew all about real life. To borrow a phrase from Charles Dickens, "It was the best of times; it was the worst of times."

Job was a good man, wealthy and respected in his community, and blessed with a close-knit family. More important, he was spiritually sensitive, as indicated by the sacrifices he offered regularly on behalf of his children.

But in four rapid-fire disasters, this good man lost everything—livestock, servants, and children. Only the messengers, the bearers of the bad tidings, survived. As one was speaking, another would arrive, each tragic news flash crashing like a giant wave against the shoreline. One after another, they broke over Job, rocking him from his surefooted stance, leaving him reeling emotionally, mentally, physically. Just as the news of the first messenger was sinking in, Job was hit with another bad report, worse than the one before.

Hearing these events described in more contemporary terms may make them more relevant. Job may not have received the news of financial disaster and loss from the morning paper; the telephone did not ring, bringing the message of his children's death; nor did a physician look over lab reports to explain his illness (Job 2). But it was all that—and more—with no time to recover before the next devastating piece of news. Each of these events was like a ten on the Richter scale; combined, they were overwhelming.

Let's take another look. First, there was the news of the

marauding Sabeans, Bedouins from Arabia, who stole Job's oxen and donkeys and killed his servants. The second messenger reported the fire of God (probably lightning) that destroyed both sheep and more servants. A Chaldean raiding party stole camels and took out still more servants, according to the third messenger.

If we read this account with the agricultural mind-set of Job's day, we realize that wealth was measured in terms of livestock—sheep, camels, oxen, and donkeys—and servants. Let's call the sheep his "stock portfolio," the camels and donkeys his transportation fleet, and the oxen his farm machinery. Let's think of his servants as employees. All those who worked for him—with the exception of the three who had brought the terrible news—had been killed. Job suffered financial setback and the loss of his entire labor force.

But a greater tragedy is yet to be played out. The last of these messengers was like the phone call in the middle of the night. As if it were not enough to lose property and workers, now Job learns that all ten of his beloved children have been wiped out in a sudden and unexpected storm. Only one servant has escaped to deliver the news. "Overnight," as Philip Yancey writes, "the greatest man in all the East was reduced to the most pitiable."[1]

We know this story well. Job's patience in suffering. Satan's wager. The counselors who come with words that fail to comfort. God's greatness in restoring to Job all that he has lost. At least, we know the facts. But in reading the familiar, we may miss the fantastic!

On His Face before God (vv. 20–21)

What we may miss is this startling statement: "At this, Job got up and tore his robe and shaved his head. Then he fell to the ground in worship" (v. 20).

Amazing, isn't it? This is not an act of despair. Typical of the day, Job's grief was demonstrated in torn clothing and a shorn head, symbols of the rending of his soul, the shearing of his life. But when he touched his face to the earth in a gesture of adoration, he was worshiping! It was real worship happening in real life, prompted by the realization that whether it is the best of times or the worst of times, God is to be praised.

We may ask how anyone could worship at such times. Job himself answers the question: "Naked I came from my mother's womb, and naked I will depart. The LORD gave and the LORD has taken away; may the name of the LORD be praised" (v. 21). Those words reveal Job's eternal perspective. This life to him was only temporary, so he kept his focus on eternity and trusted fully in the sovereign God. As Charles Spurgeon wrote, "When you go through a trial, the sovereignty of God is the pillow upon which you lay your head." Job knew that pillow.

For Job, worship was real, as much a part of him as his next breath. For us, worship may be Sundays only, with the rest of the week spent in scrambling for survival. Which do you prefer—the Sunday-go-to-meeting variety, or the worship that can steel your soul? If it is the once-a-week dose, hopefully enough to inoculate you from guilt, or an appetizer you're hoping will fill you like a fast-food meal grabbed at the drive-through window, then this book is not for you.

On the other hand, if you're looking for a change—one that will impact your corporate worship experience, revitalize your quiet times, and infuse every aspect of your life with the presence of God, then read on, with this book in one hand and your Bible in the other.

If your definition of worship is a Sunday-only observance; if you need a certain brand of music or demand a predictable order of service, then you are missing the fullness of all God intended worship to be. Worship should be woven into the very fabric of our lives, so that whatever happens and whenever it happens, we live on our faces before God.

Making It Real

In 1636, amid the darkness of the Thirty-Year War, a German pastor, Martin Rinkart, is said to have buried five thousand of his parishioners in one year, an average of fifteen a day. In those perilous times, his parish was ravaged by war, death, and economic disaster. In the heart of that darkness, with fear on his doorstep, he sat down and wrote this table grace for his children:

> Now thank we all our God With heart and hands and voices,
>
> Who wondrous things hath done, In whom His world rejoices.
>
> Who, from our mother's arms, Hath blessed us on our way
>
> With countless gifts of love, And still is ours today.

Martin Rinkart knew how to make worship real. He knew how to take worship, real worship, into real life. In the worst of times he could praise God for the wondrous things He had done. We can learn to do that too.

As you read this book, you will need:

• **The Word of God.** True worship will not be learned apart from God's Word. Anything else will be a substitute — unacceptable, temporary, and ultimately doomed to fail. Most chapters of this book will begin with a biblical reference. Read the passage and pray, asking God to help you understand what He is trying to teach you about worship.

• **The Holy Spirit.** It is God's Spirit who teaches, convicts, encourages, and leads us into all truth. Only He can help us live the faith life to which Jesus calls us.

• **Commitment.** We can read God's Word, hear His Spirit whispering to our hearts, feel convicted, and still miss the whole point. This adventure will take work and a commitment to put into practice what we learn. We must do more than learn about worship — we must live it.

What prompts you to worship God? Has it become rote and ritual . . . or do you allow real-life situations, like Job's and Martin Rinkart's, to move you into a place of praise?

To the casual observer, we may look like true worshipers. We may practice church attendance, pray before meals and meetings, even make regular donations to the work of the Lord. Yet an Old Testament prophet dared to condemn the worshipers of his day, people who also observed the "letter of the Law." He condemned them, as we will see in the next chapter, for worshiping in form only and not with the heart.

GOING DEEPER
(A Personal Study Guide)

Part 1—Getting into the Word

Prayer—As you begin this study, ask God to speak to you through His Word. Make it your goal not only to learn what the Bible has to say about worship but to understand what it means for you today. Ask God to give you a passionate desire to know Him as Job knew Him.

Reading/Hearing God's Word—Read or listen to Job 1. Watch for verses or ideas that are especially meaningful to you. In particular, look for things that relate to either "real life" or "real worship." Force your thinking off your usual habit trail and let God's Word begin to redefine worship for you.

Understanding God's Word—Read the chapter again. Underline any key phrases or ideas. Then answer the following questions:

1. In what ways was this period of Job's life both "the best of times and the worst of times"?

_____

_____

_____

2. Job's worship is demonstrated in what actions and words?

_____

_____

_____

Meditating on God's Word—Write a brief summary of a meaningful verse or idea you noticed:

_____

_____

_____

Part 2—The Word in Review

Introduction

Job's story retold

I. The Agony and the Ecstasy (Job 1:13–19)

A. It was the best of times

Good man, wealthy, respected, close-knit family, spiritually sensitive

B. It was the worst of times

Rapid-fire disasters:

1. Home robbed (twice)

2. Livestock destroyed

3. Fatal accident

II. On His Face before God (1:20–21)

A. The outward symbols of the inward anguish

Torn clothes, shaved head

B. The inward response demonstrated in the outward actions

Job fell to the ground in worship

Part 3—Taking the Word into My World

Does Job's story sound familiar? I hope that retelling this story in contemporary language has given it new relevance. Recall some of the "tough times" you have endured. List several.

_____

_____

_____

Now draw the contrast. How did you respond? Before reading this chapter, if someone had asked you, "What prompts you to worship?" what would your answer have been?

_____

_____

_____

Read again the paragraph on page 21 that begins with this statement: "We may ask how anyone could worship at such times." What are the two reasons Job could worship in the worst of times?

1._____

2._____

Describe in your own words what it means to put everything in an eternal perspective. In what ways does the sovereignty of God help you worship in the tough times?

_____

_____

_____

Part 4—Grabbing Hold

We are created to worship God. The important thing is to realize that worship is not just a church activity but a way of life. Do you really want to develop the heart God desires and learn to give worship not just more of your life but to make it the core of your life—all the time?

CHAPTER 2

STOP THE MUSIC

Isaiah 1:1–20

"Worship has become a commodity . . . we can become so interested in doing things 'right' to get the 'right' response from people that we miss the whole point."
—Tom Kraeuter

And God said, "Stop the music," but no one was really listening. They were too caught up in their rituals to hear what He had to say about worship. After all, there were offerings to collect, services to attend, prayers to be prayed.

Is this the picture at your house on Sunday morning? First one to the car honks the horn, signaling that the others better hurry or they'll be late. And there's the designated heel-dragger. She would have come sooner if she could have found the mate to her Sunday shoes.

The atmosphere is tense until the car pulls into the church parking lot. Then it's all smiles and cheerful greetings on the way into the building. In the hallway, people pass without really seeing each other, speak without saying anything. We're simply putting in time, eager to get on with other weekend activities.

In the pew, we sit quietly with eyes closed, minds racing. Praying for some missionary who is several thousand miles away seems appropriate for people whose minds have wandered a similar distance from the place of worship.

Rewind the tape to another time, another culture. An ancient people who claim to know God are also going through the motions of worship. Let's listen in on their argument.

A Rebellious Nation (vv. 1–9)

Like the bailiff calling the court to order, Isaiah cries out, "Hear, O heavens! Listen, O earth!" (v. 2). The trial is about to begin; the plaintiff is God Himself, who brings accusations against His own people. The charge? Worthless worship—and He wants it stopped. A divine injunction is being issued.

Why would God stop His people when they are doing what appears to be what He wants—giving, attending, praying? Yet that's exactly what happened in Isaiah 1, a chapter that expresses divine disgust with worship when it is all form and no function, an emphasis on doing and not being, a routine that focuses on the art instead of the heart.

The Book of Isaiah was written during a stormy period in the history of Israel. While the Assyrian empire was expanding, Israel was in a period of decline. It is God's mercy alone, the prophet says, that has kept the nation from the total destruction it deserves.

Isaiah knew how the people would react to his message. He expected that they would protest God's judgment, citing in their defense their diligent worship as evidence. "How could God condemn us when we're only doing what He told us to do?"

Yet their acts of worship, their best defense, were repulsive to God. What Isaiah writes in response should challenge us to examine our own motives to determine whether we are focusing on the art or the heart of worship.

God Rejects the Art of Worship (vv. 10–15)

Isaiah's opening words ring with an imagery that should have made the people recoil in horror. The prophet compares the Israelites to cities so wicked that God wiped them off the face of the earth. "Hear the word of the LORD, you rulers of Sodom; listen to the law of our God, you people of Gomorrah!" (v. 10). At Abraham's request, God would have spared these cities if only ten righteous people had been found.

To this day Sodom and Gomorrah are remembered for their sinfulness. So Isaiah's comparison—that God's people are the embodiment of evil—should have rattled their collective consciousness. But it did not.

Isaiah then moved beyond what might be dismissed as name-calling and got specific. He showed them God's opinion of their worship practices.

The sacrifices. In their defense the children of Israel reminded the Almighty of their faithful observance of the rituals. There were so many of them that Isaiah would speak of "the multitude" of their sacrifices. God's reply? A divine shrug of the shoulder. "'What are they to me?" (v. 11).

God was not repudiating the sacrifices He had commanded. As we read the Old Testament, especially the Book of Leviticus, we find the detailed instructions God gave to His people. The work of the Levitical priests was never done. In contrast, the sacrifice of Jesus atoned for all sins of all time; no further sacrifices are necessary (Heb. 10:14). So why, centuries before the death of Christ, would Isaiah condemn the people for being obedient to God's command?

Their sacrifices were rejected because *right acts from wrong hearts are never acceptable to God*. Even proper forms of worship offend Him when they are merely forms followed, offerings presented by unrepentant worshipers seeking not to worship but to spare themselves the just punishment of their sins. When such sacrifices are offered only to appease God, they amount to nothing more than bribery.

"Enough," God said. "I have more than enough of burnt offerings, of rams and the fat of fattened animals; I have no pleasure in the blood of bulls and lambs and goats" (v. 11). What should have been an aroma pleasing to the Lord, a fragrant offering, was a stench in His nostrils. How could something intended to be so right go so wrong?

The religious festivals. God also had instructed His people to observe certain feast days and festivals as reminders of His mercy and His provision. There were the annual feasts, such as Passover, Pentecost, and Tabernacles (Ex. 23:14–17; 34:18–25; Lev. 23; Deut. 16:1–17), and there were special feasts such as those described in Numbers 28:11–15: "On the first of every month, present to the LORD a burnt offering" (v. 11).

29

The people had kept this command "religiously." After all, isn't this what God wanted? Yes and no. Yes, He wanted Israel to worship Him. But no, He did not want worship to become a shadowy form with no substance. Instead of a reverent approach to God, the temple gatherings are described in Isaiah 1 as the "trampling of my courts" (v. 12). Meeting with God had become a meaningless rite.

Listen to God's condemnation of these acts: "Your incense is detestable to me. New Moons, Sabbaths and convocations—I cannot bear your evil assemblies. Your New Moon festivals and your appointed feasts my soul hates. They have become a burden to me; I am weary of bearing them" (vv. 13–14). Strong words—"detestable incense," "evil assemblies," "weary," "hate," "burden"—reveal the intensity of God's emotion toward shallow worship.

The people were doing the right things—for the wrong reasons. To say that God was not pleased is putting it mildly. He wanted to put an end to this farce; He couldn't bear it; He hated what they were doing. There was no value in coming before Him with hearts that were unyielded and disobedient.

The prayers. Not only did God reject this mockery, but He would not listen to the prayers of His people. Shocking? Maybe, but God is serious about worship. "When you spread out your hands in prayer, I will hide my eyes from you; even if you offer many prayers, I will not listen" (v. 15). Their "multitude" of words could not open God's ears. He closed off all communication. Why?

To help us grasp the significance of this comment, let's remember that in supplicatory prayer, the Hebrews extended their hands with the palms upward toward God. As you picture a person standing to pray in this position, look closely, and you will understand God's refusal to listen. "Your hands are full of blood" (v. 15). What a travesty. That worshipers would lift hands stained with the blood of the innocent victims they have oppressed or even killed!

Iniquities and sins separate people from God so that He will not hear their prayers, Isaiah later told the Israelites

(59:1–2). Failure to turn from their sins had rendered these worshipers utterly filthy before God.

The lesson for us today? Just because we pray doesn't mean God has to listen. He expects much more than empty words.

These ancient people had mastered the art of worship. They had multiplied the number of sacrifices, religiously kept the feasts and festivals, and spread their hands before God in prayer—yet none of it was acceptable or pleasing to Him. Their sacrifices stank, their festivals were no more than milling crowds without purpose, and their prayers were a sham. God was sick of the whole deal. His indictment complete, Isaiah presses the argument, not for a conviction, but for change.

God Desires the Heart of Worship (vv. 16–20)

Isaiah was part prophet, part cardiologist, and part medical examiner. He knew that before worship can be adjusted, the heart must change. True worship is a matter of the heart.

What God desired the people do is presented in its simplest terms in these verses: "Repent and do right." These two actions flow from the heart.

A change of mind. First, Isaiah instructs the people in repentance: "Stop doing wrong" (v. 16). They are to wash and make themselves clean. "Take your evil deeds out of my sight!" God says to them through His prophet. This is not a change in the order of service—how their worship was conducted—but a change on the inside that will make their worship acceptable.

God had decreed special protection for the widows and orphans, yet they were among those who suffered from the social injustices and oppression of the people. The wrong done them was obvious, repulsive to God, and rendered the people unfit for worship. It had to stop.

Yet it is not only a stop-what-you-are-doing kind of instruction. It is replacing wrong with right, as Paul wrote to the church at Ephesus (Eph. 4:25). So to the people of Judah, Isaiah says, "Stop doing wrong, learn to do right!" (vv. 16–17).

The door was not closed to true worship, but held wide open by the God who sends a message more beautiful and enduring than any found on a greeting card: "'Come now, let us *reason* together,' says the LORD. 'Though your sins are like scarlet, they shall be as white as snow; though they are red as crimson, they shall be like wool'" (v. 18). What an invitation! The Lord asks the people to be reasonable, to talk things over with Him in order to come to a conclusion.

Then He proceeds to stretch their minds. He suggests that it is actually possible for their lives, stained with the reddest possible dye, to become, through His mercy, the purest white. The scarlet dyes of Bible times would have left an indelible mark on any fabric. Yet it is just that imagery that Isaiah uses to emphasize the completeness of God's forgiveness. A life so stained as to appear permanently marred could experience a soul-cleansing, like a garment of crimson becoming as wool.

With this incredible promise before them as inspiration, they need to make up their minds to live in holiness. And to launch this revised agenda, the prophet offers a to-do list: Seek justice, encourage the oppressed, defend the cause of the fatherless, plead the case of the widow (v. 17). Living in holiness will result in actions that flow from hearts made right with God.

A change of heart. Change doesn't happen overnight. You don't just get up one morning and find that all is well. Inspired by the Holy Spirit, the Convicter, it takes a moment of decision, followed by determination to stick with His protocol until the desired change occurs.

In their vain attempt to worship, God's people had been going through the motions. Now it is time to get real. The next two verses drive home the point with the classic "if you are willing . . . but" construction.

God was holding the door open. If they were willing to be obedient, His blessing would be theirs. But if they continued to resist and rebel, judgment would follow.

True worship is not a matter of being in the right place at the right time, of saying the right things, and singing the right songs. Throughout the centuries, like the people of Isaiah's day, worshipers have presented such acts as evidence of worship. Even Jesus spoke of a day when people would offer their actions as evidence in their defense when He said, "Many will say to me on that day, 'Lord, Lord, did we not prophesy in your name, and in your name drive out demons and perform many miracles?'" (Matt. 7:22).

Will we ever learn?

Hungry Hearts

In a hot-off-the press (as of this printing) survey of a random sampling of regular church attendees, 92 percent said they believe that worship is the most important of all church-based experiences, including learning about faith, moral and spiritual accountability, and serving the poor and disenfranchised. Paradoxically, however, at least two-thirds of this number feel that they do not always experience the presence of God at church.

Why? Partly because we do not have a clear understanding of worship as a matter of the heart. This survey also revealed that many churchgoers do not make worship a daily exercise, but merely work it into their weekend plans with no preparation beforehand.

"Without giving themselves time to clear their minds and hearts of their daily distractions and other problems, many people attend a worship event but never enter a worshipful frame of mind," says George Barna, who directed the research. "A large share of churchgoers do not pray, meditate, confess or focus on God prior to the start of a church worship event. One consequence is that they find it difficult to connect with Him spiritually. Having never been taught much about worship, they find the inability to interact with God on a deeper level frustrating, but don't know what to do about it."[1]

This is modern testimony to the truth of Isaiah. Worship is not just a thing we do, a place to go, prayers we pray, and offerings we give. If it were a matter of familiar habit trails, people would find satisfaction in the services they attend. But if they do not, it is because they are not worshiping from the heart.

Making It Real

Isaiah pointed to the art of worship practiced by God's people—sacrifices, festivals, prayers. Think through your own daily agenda. What outward acts characterize your worship? (Or is it a Sunday-morning-only event?) If you are having difficulty in making such a list, ask yourself, "If someone wanted to convict me of being a worshiper, what evidence could they find?"

Remember, worship is not just a matter of *what you do* but *who you are*. Jesus said, "No one comes to the Father except through me" (John 14:6). Are you a believer? Have you received Jesus as Savior for the forgiveness of your sins? Remember how you were unable to get the spilled red punch out of the carpet? Neither can you remove the scarlet stain of sin from your life. But God can. By His mercy and grace, through the death of His Son on that crimson cross, your eternal salvation was bought with a great price.

Notice that when Isaiah instructed the people in what needed to change, he pointed to their sins. "Take your evil deeds out of my sight!" (v. 16). The people's wrongdoing kept their worship from being acceptable to God.

If you are as sick of your sin as God is, if you desire to have clean hands and a pure heart (Ps. 24:4), pray the prayer of David: "Search me, O God, and know my heart; test me and know my anxious thoughts. See if there is any offensive way in me, and lead me in the way everlasting" (139:23–24).

But don't pray this prayer if you don't mean business. God will take you at your word and clearly define where change is needed in your life. It may not be a pretty sight!

Still, if you are serious about interacting with God, here are some tips for making worship real:

• Consciously think about the songs you sing. Consider the words and make them the prayer of your heart.

• Join in the prayers of others. As you hear the requests, add your acknowledgment with a nod of the head or a whispered "amen."

• Show how you value God's Word by paying careful attention to the lessons taught. Taking notes will not only help you remember the message, but will also force you to concentrate.

Putting all of this together—along with living your worship when you leave—will help "the art" reflect "the heart." When the benediction is given and the meeting is over, the service should just be beginning.

GOING DEEPER
(A Personal Study Guide)

Part 1—Getting into the Word

Prayer—As you pray, ask God to help you understand Isaiah's scathing denunciation of Israel's worship practices. Use that standard to evaluate your own. We may want to apply a bandage when open-heart surgery is needed, so be willing to let God probe as deeply as necessary.

Reading/Hearing God's Word—Read Isaiah 1. Look for verses or ideas that are especially important for this time in your life. In particular, be aware of words that indicate God's assessment of Israel's worship.

Understanding God's Word—Reread the chapter. Underline key phrases and ideas. Then tackle the following assignment:

1. Scan the passage (vv. 1–20), listing the words Isaiah used to catch the attention of the people.

_____

_____

_____

2. Do any of them apply to your approach to worship? If so, which ones?

_____

_____

_____

Meditating on God's Word—Read Matthew 15:7–9 and write a brief summary of these verses, using words and phrases that would challenge worshipers today.

_____

_____

_____

What would Jesus say if He were speaking to a twenty-first century audience?

_____

_____

_____

Part 2—The Word in Review

Introduction

God said, "Stop the music," but no one was really listening. Sometimes people are just going through the motions of worship, and God is not pleased. He loves us enough to challenge our motives so that our worship will be pure.

I. God Rejects the Art of Worship (Isa. 1:1–15)

    A. The sacrifices (v. 11)
    B. The religious festivals (vv. 12–14)
    C. The prayers (v. 15)

II. God Desires the Heart of Worship (1:16–20)

    A. A change of mind (v. 16)
    B. A change of heart (vv. 19–20)

Part 3—Taking the Word into My World

This powerful passage from Isaiah should force us to examine closely our acts of worship, both private and public. To help apply this lesson to real life today, note the parallels between Isaiah's day and ours in each of the major areas addressed in these verses:

Your sacrifices (offerings). How do you give? How much do you give? Does getting a tax deduction for your gift make a significant difference to you? Should it?

_____
_____
_____

Your worship attendance. How often do you attend worship services? Do you maintain a consistent personal prayer life? How important is it to you? What is your attitude when you get alone with God for devotions or when driving to church?

_____
_____
_____

Your prayers. When you pray, does God hear the same kind of meaningless repetition Jesus rebuked in Matthew 6:7?

_____
_____
_____

The change needed among Old Testament worshipers was not merely a change of actions, but one that begins with a change of heart. Notice that when the heart change fueled life change, more than offerings, festivals, and prayers were affected (Isa. 1:16–17). How does this reinforce the teaching that real worship affects real life?

_____
_____
_____

Part 4—Grabbing Hold

Read Matthew 6. In this passage Jesus addresses some of the same issues Isaiah addressed centuries earlier. Combine Isaiah's list and Jesus' list. Then pray, asking God to help you see which issues apply to your worship. Ask God to help you develop a heart like His.

_____
_____
_____

Determine to keep reading, studying, praying, and changing. Diagnosis comes before treatment. Treatment comes before healing, and sometimes the treatment hurts. But pain often precedes a positive outcome. No pain, no gain!

CHAPTER 3

WHEN THE BAND WAS BANNED

Isaiah 1:10–20

*"In the end, worship can never be a performance,
something you're pretending or putting on. It's got to be an
overflow of your heart . . . . Worship is about getting personal
with God, drawing close to God."*
—Matt Redman

The pastor said, "The band is banned," and the people listened. It was not time for another "sound check" but for a heart check at Soul Survivor Church in Watford, England.

The church, a youthful congregation, was meeting in a new building with a state-of-the-art sound system. The worship leader, Matt Redman, was widely known and respected. Their ministry was reaching people around the world, yet something was "up."

Their worship, too, was state-of-the-art. As Pastor Mike Pilavachi put it, with a wry twist of humor, "On the surface everything was just fine; . . . the musicians had worked out how to tune their instruments and the sound engineers were getting out of bed on time." On a more serious note, he added, "Each service contained a block of songs that focused on the cross and gave people the chance to get down to business with God. To make this easier, the music was (nearly) up-to-date, the chairs had disappeared, and the lights were low: what better atmosphere for young people to worship God?"[1]

They were singing the songs, but something was missing. These were worshipers who had become "connoisseurs" of praise instead of participants. So the band was banned.

In the following weeks, worship was led with only one acoustic guitar, sometimes with vocal music only, and finally with no musical accompaniment at all. When all the props were removed, they could see where their hearts were. At times, there were awkward periods of silence because no one had a sacrifice of praise to bring. It was a painful process, but a necessary one.

In time, with all the comforts of their familiar form of worship gone and without the emotional boost of the band, this church again found the heart of worship.

Out of that season of soul-searching at Soul Survivor came a song, written by Matt Redman—a member of the banned band—expressing his heart:

When the music fades,
All is stripped away,
And I simply come.
Longing just to bring
Something that's of worth
That will bless Your heart.

I'll bring You more than a song.
For a song in itself is not what
You have required.
You search much deeper within,
Through the way things appear;
You're looking into my heart.

I'm coming back to the heart of worship,
And it's all about You,
All about You, Jesus.
I'm sorry, Lord, for the thing I've made it.
When it's all about You. All about You, Jesus.

(Matt Redman ©1997 Kingsway's Thankyou Music)

When the Music Fades

One of the *positive* things that is happening in churches today is a renewed interest in and emphasis on worship. One of the *negative* things that is happening in churches today is a renewed interest in and emphasis on worship. Strange as it may seem, these two statements are not contradictory.

That's because not everybody talking about worship is doing it. For that matter, many people using the word *worship* don't really know what it means. Worse still, there is a significant amount of conflict, disagreement, and division over issues related to how we should or should not worship.

Some of us raised in the free-church tradition may remember the sameness of our services. For years it was basically hymn, prayer, hymn, announcements, offering, choir, hymn, sermon, hymn, and prayer. In this approach to corporate worship, typically everything that took place before the sermon was preliminary to the main event—the preaching. Yes, we were free—to repeat the same formula every week.

Then the attention turned to worship. Some of us moved from that repetitive model to a model that encouraged people to enter into all aspects of the service with an attitude of worship. The format of preliminaries and preaching was phased out, replaced by a unified theme where the elements blended together, every part having a carefully thought-out purpose. This is good. God desires our worship when it is not just rote and routine but an expression of the heart. The interest in and emphasis on worship is a positive.

At the same time there are some negative aspects to worship as we know it. The main contributors to this dark side of worship are the lack of a correct definition of real worship and disagreements as to how to go about worshiping. People are planning worship events, attending worship services, singing worship songs—as they would describe and define the term. But unless worship conforms to God's definition, it is worship in name only. A biblical understanding is absolutely essential.

We may use the latest technology available—large-screen displays and sound enhancements—and still not worship. We may have the creative synergy to blend and utilize a variety of instruments—and still not worship. The flow of the service may have been carefully scripted, integrating all of the elements into a unity that blends with the sermon—and it is still not worship.

What is needed is a theology of worship. Theology must precede methodology. We must know what the Bible teaches, understand it correctly, and then build our worship upon that foundation.

Worship Is a Verb

"The difference between a biblical and a pagan understanding of worship lies in the difference between a verb and a noun," says Ben Patterson in an article published in *Leadership Journal*.[2]

Think back to your early school days, when you were learning English grammar. A noun names a person, place, or thing. To speak of worship as a service to be attended is to use the word *worship* as a noun, much as we would speak of going to a ball game. Worship becomes an event to watch, a place to go, and worshipers, the spectators in the stands. If this is our experience of worship, then we have, as Patterson would say, a pagan understanding of it, and we fall far short of God's intent.

In contrast, a verb is a word that expresses an action. *Worship*, a verb? Yes, in the sense that worship is something you *do*, not something you *watch*.

Dig a little deeper, and you will find that the most common Old Testament Hebrew word for *worship* means "to bow down, to do homage." In the New Testament, the Greek language carries the same meaning: "to bow down," "to serve." These are actions. Put it all together, and the Bible clearly points to the fact that worship involves doing as well as being.

When *worship* is understood as a verb, it is viewed not as an event to watch or a place to go but as something the worshiper does. It is action, attitude, and offering all flowing out of a life that desires to give praise, adoration, and glory to

God. When we think of it as something in which we participate, our comprehension moves from a pagan to a biblical understanding of the word.

My favorite definition of worship is stated by Warren Wiersbe in his book *Real Worship:* "Worship is the believer's response of all that he is—mind, emotions, will and body—to all that God is and says and does."[3] This definition, with elements we will explore later, emphasizes *worship* as a verb. Worship is an active response to the majesty of God.

This brings us back to the problem of *worship* as a noun. If worship were a thing, then the emphasis would be on the art of worship. Since *worship* is a verb—actions resulting from attitude—then it is the heart of worship that matters.

The Thing We've Made It

Wouldn't you think that worship would draw people closer to God and closer together? That we would always feel the sweet presence of His Spirit? That we would then move on, refreshed and blessed, ready to tackle all of life's problems, confident of victory?

This is certainly God's intent for His children, but unfortunately, it is not always the case. In fact, the place of prayer and praise can become a place of conflict, division, and disagreement. So much so, that the term "worship wars" is now a part of the vocabulary of the church!

Tensions often arise when new worship styles are introduced. It's as if some people can only worship in a certain setting, with a certain format. The service becomes consumer-oriented, giving the people what they want, rather than seeking to determine what pleases God.

We shouldn't be surprised. What God desires, Satan disrupts. God desires worship that unites His people and glorifies His name. Satan has effectively made worship divisive, drawing attention away from God and giving the glory to the performers instead.

Satan has never been a stranger to worship, as Ezekiel 28 reveals: "'full of wisdom and perfect in beauty,'" he was foremost among God's creatures (v. 12). As a cherub, his responsibilities included guarding the holiness and majesty of God, a ministry carried out in the presence of God Himself.

But pride and selfish ambition began to overtake him. Isaiah elaborates, telling of Satan's plot against God. Five times he uses the phrase "I will" to describe Satan's plan (Isa. 14:13–14). Apparently his intent was to take over God's domain. "I will make myself like the Most High," he boasted (v. 14).

Satan's sin—pride—set him in opposition to God. Pride desires to take from God the attention and glory that belong to Him alone.

As you explore what the Word of God teaches about worship, examine your heart. What God desires is worship that begins within. Without a right heart, there can be no right worship.

Making It Real

Perhaps getting back to the heart of worship for you will involve stripping away all the externals and extras. As you gather for times of corporate worship, force yourself to look beyond the things that can be seen and heard, and focus on the God you worship.

Our family learned a great lesson on heart preparation from a brief feature on the radio. Now, as we drive to church, we know that at a particular intersection we will begin to pray. Everyone in the car takes a turn, praying for the pastors, Sunday school teachers, and our part in the worship, fellowship, and instruction of the day. We also use the time to pray for other ministries and friends with special needs.

While you may not be able to strip away all the excess from your times of corporate worship, you can more easily simplify your times alone with God.

• Find a quiet place.

• Take your Bible and perhaps a songbook or devotional book, and set aside time for worship.

• In the solitude of these moments, when you cannot hide behind forms or formats, pray the lyric of Matt Redman's song:

> I'm coming back to the heart of worship,
>
> And it's all about You,
>
> All about You, Jesus.
>
> I'm sorry, Lord, for the thing I've made it.
>
> When it's all about You,
>
> All about You, Jesus.

GOING DEEPER
(A Personal Study Guide)

Part 1—Getting into the Word

Prayer— After working through chapter 2, you know that routine, insincere prayer is not God's idea of worship. He does, however, want you to spend time with Him, both in a group and one-on-one. Allow for moments of silence, no matter how awkward they might feel. Listen to what His heart is speaking to your heart.

Reading/Hearing God's Word—Read or listen to Isaiah 22:12-13, observing the prophet's call for change and the people's inappropriate response. These verses remind us that change comes from the heart and that God takes note of our refusals to change.

Understanding God's Word—Notice again the key words or ideas that you underlined in your previous study of this passage. Review your notes of group discussions. Do the same with the list constructed when you compared Isaiah 1 with Matthew 6.

Meditating on God's Word—This is your second time through these verses. Ponder the outstanding verse that captures God's heart for you (Isa. 1:18). Memorize His promise to forgive you when you fail to measure up.

Part 2—The Word in Review

In this continuation of the study of Isaiah 1, the opening story gives the background of a popular contemporary Christian song, "Heart of Worship." If possible, find a CD or tape of this song, as sung by the composer, Matt Redman, and play it in your quiet times. Knowing the story behind the song will enhance the meaning of the words.

Practice your memory work whenever you have a moment. Allow the refreshing words of this verse to remind you that even when you, like the ancient Israelites, are stubborn and rebellious, God is patient and longsuffering.

Part 3—Taking the Word into My World

List some of the positive things you have noticed in your worship—both corporately and privately:

_____

_____

_____

List some of the negatives:

_____

_____

_____

Reflect on this statement: "It should not surprise us that there are so many disagreements regarding worship. God desires worship—and what God desires, Satan disrupts."

Read again Warren Wiersbe's definition of worship. Using this definition as a standard, study each aspect to measure your spiritual temperature.

1. Worship is a matter of the heart.

2. Worship is about God, not us.

3. Worship affects our entire life.

Part 4—Grabbing Hold

I was on my way to speak at a church one morning when the radio station I was listening to played Matt Redman singing "Heart of Worship." Knowing the story behind the song had already affected how I responded when I heard others sing it. But hearing it sung and performed by the composer really moved me.

As you close this study time, listen to the song as recorded by Matt Redman, if possible. If not, read the words as a prayer.

CHAPTER 4

THE CHANGE AGENT

Isaiah 6

"God is not moved or impressed with our worship until our hearts are moved and impressed by Him."
—Kelly Sparks

How do you change the human heart? Nothing dietary, physiological, pharmaceutical, or surgical about it. The way to change the heart is through worship.

To be like Job, who worshiped in the worst of times, might seem impossible, something only an Old Testament saint could pull off. Certainly not a twenty-first century sophisticate, who lives with the expectation of health care, environmental protection, and financial planning. In a culture shaped by the media—images of health and beauty, pleasure and instant gratification—serious trouble often seems remote. But when it comes . . . would we worship?

Sure, worship may be more habit trail than holiness. The routine becomes a rut. Every seven days another Sunday appears on the calendar, and we switch into worship mode.

Still, God is not anti-routine or even anti-ritual. A reading of Leviticus can dispel that notion rather quickly. The only real question is this: How can worship bring about the coronary catharsis that results in real heart change?

It was a time very much like today—a time of prosperity and sinful pride. The leader of the country had been instrumental in orchestrating an era of stability. With everything under control, the king could focus on building the economy, taking care of the needs of people, creating a sense of national security. In spite of these blessings, the result was not gratitude to God but an amazing arrogance on the part of the king.

But then he died. The immediate vacuum in leadership was filled with a sense of uncertainty, and the nation began to experience change.

It was at that precise moment that another man came on the scene—a man with a message, a searing, even scathing denunciation. A man who was not afraid to stand before the people and tell the truth. Not intimidated by either the times or the difficulty of his task, Isaiah the prophet spoke the Word of God.

Not all prophets respond to God's commission as this man did. Elijah fled to the desert. Jonah headed in the opposite direction. Even Moses, initially, tried to beg off. But not Isaiah. God captured his attention—in an hour of worship.

In Worship There Is Revelation: Seeing God as He Is (vv. 1–4)

Isaiah was sent to people who ridiculed the One who had sent him. "Let God hurry, let him hasten his work so we may see it," they mocked. "Let it approach, let the plan of the Holy One of Israel come, so we may know it" (5:19). Beneath this smooth talk was the real truth—an intent to demean and denigrate God Himself.

Oh, they wanted to hear what Isaiah had to say because the prophet could tell them, firsthand, about the Holy One of Israel. Isaiah was a credible witness. He had been transformed by a revelation God had given him.

Exactly what did this man see that was powerful enough to change his life forever?

He saw the Lord. In a vision, Isaiah saw God enthroned in the midst of the glories of heaven. The earthly king, Uzziah, had died, but the true King of the Universe still reigned supreme. The words "high and exalted" rightly describe God, as do their synonyms: "above all, lifted up, lofty, elevated, preeminent, ruling, chief, towering, noble, powerful, foremost." God echoes Isaiah in His own words: "I live in a high and holy place" (57:15).

In the throne room of heaven, God is seated, as befits the King of kings. When a ruling monarch is present, all stand, and only the king sits. In Revelation 4, John's vision, the elders leave their seats to worship the One who is sitting on the throne (v. 10).

When this description of God's grandeur and majesty truly penetrates our souls, we will realize that the Lord is far greater than any king or potentate who has ever lived. This is not a Being who is to be treated as a cosmic errand-runner, One who exists to do our will if we pray with the right fervor or formula. He is high and exalted—we are not. Isaiah saw Him as He truly is.

He heard the praise. After describing the vision before him, Isaiah tells of the seraphs, angelic beings, who were calling to one another. The name of this group of angels is taken from the Hebrew word that means "to burn," a graphic way of expressing the zealousness of their worship. They use their six wings to cover their faces and feet while flying before God. In humility, they are unable to look upon Him. In reverence, they hide their feet. In readiness to serve Him, they use their other pair of wings to fly. There is no hint of casualness in their worship. They are completely attentive, energized, humble, and reverent. Understanding who God is, acknowledging His majesty and holiness, these beings are consumed with praise in the presence of God.

As the seraphs call to one another like a great antiphonal choir, the throne room rings with the sound of their voices, and Isaiah's heart is stirred by the words of their song: "Holy, holy, holy is the LORD Almighty; the whole earth is full of His glory" (v. 3).

The threefold repetition emphasizes God's holiness, His "set-apartness." Isaiah heard the song of the angels and wanted Israel to know that God, above all else, is absolute holiness.

"Holy is the LORD Almighty." The redemptive name of God—LORD—is used, along with a description of His attributes. The LORD God is neither a regional deity nor Someone whose ultimate will can be thwarted. Rather, He is the

Almighty, the omnipotent, the immutable God of the universe who is everywhere present.

So powerful is He that we cannot escape His presence (Ps. 139:7). The whole earth is full of the glory of the transcendent God. Everywhere we go, all of creation shouts His praises (19:1–4). Holy, Almighty, transcendent—a trilogy of attributes reveals the nature of God in this scene of celestial worship.

◆

For worship to be what God intends it to be, for worship to change the heart of the worshiper, the focus must be on Him.

While some criticize the worship music of recent years, an interesting commendation comes from John Piper, who writes: "An unmistakable trend in the worship songs is this: they are, by and large, and in a new way, God-ward . . . [they] address God in the second person. They are sung to God directly, not merely to each other about God. Therefore they force the issue of worship as a God-ward act—an engagement of the heart with the living God as the song is sung.

"Whatever you think of the drums, the electric guitar and bass and amplification and T-shirts and platforms cluttered with wires and mikes and speakers, it is unmistakable—the dominant theme of these songs is God—the character of God, the power of God, the mercy of God, the authority of God, and the fatherhood of God. And the hoped-for effect of relentlessly addressing God directly in the second person is engagement—genuine, real, spiritual engagement—if the heart is with God."[1]

We need a fresh vision of God, not a time of entertainment. When worship becomes what we want it to be, the focus is on ourselves; we may enjoy the worship times, but leave unaffected. But when God is the center of worship, when through His Word we see Him as He is, we will be changed.

With the revelation comes a realization. The upward look prompts an inward look.

In Worship There Is Realization: Seeing Ourselves as God Sees Us (vv. 5–7)

Isaiah's vision of God cleared his vision of himself. Only one response was possible: "Woe to me!" he cried. "I am ruined! For I am a man of unclean lips, and I live among a people of unclean lips" (v. 5). No defense, no attempt to justify, no excuse, no whitewashing of the truth. Isaiah knew the sin in his life and in the lives of his countrymen.

Like the leper, he cried, "Unclean, unclean!" Confronted by the holiness of God, everything else was rottenness and filth.

In a day of permissiveness, such an expression of personal unworthiness is incomprehensible. As the line between the lifestyle of the people of God and the lifestyle of the present world system is increasingly blurred, we lose sight of the truth. Unless we use God's standard of holiness, it is possible that what to Him is so wrong will to us seem so right.

Not so for Isaiah. He knew the truth about himself and his people, and he was immediately convicted. How could he hope to be near God, let alone stand in God's presence?

It is God's forgiveness that makes man's standing acceptable. The imagery of the seraph touching the prophet's mouth with a live coal from the altar is explained by the angel: "See, this has touched your lips; your guilt is taken away and your sin atoned for" (v. 7). Isaiah is now a clean vessel, one that can be used to serve God.

In true worship we see God for who He is; we then see ourselves for what we are. We need this vision of ourselves, a vision that brings the desire for the cleansing that comes from the sacrificial altar, this gift that is offered to us by the God of burning holiness Himself.

In Worship There Is Response: We Are Changed (v. 8)

True worship is not simply another site to visit on a tourist's itinerary, or a theatrical performance to watch, or a contest to view, like a spectator in a stadium seat. Sure, worship may be seen, enjoyed, and remembered, but a major difference is that true worship also produces change.

Being affected by worship involves two things. First, the worshiper must be listening. Isaiah said, "I heard." This was not a casual acknowledgment of sound in the same room—like a husband nodding as if he really is tuned in to his wife while planning his next fishing trip—but a conscious hearing, a registering of what was said. The mind was connected, the input received.

Second, the worshiper must respond—act, change, do, be—because of what has been heard. After he heard God's voice, saying, "Whom shall I send? And who will go for us?" Isaiah replied, "Here am I. Send me!" (v. 8). His response implied action that he was prepared to take.

When worship is viewed as a performance or something to occupy the attention of a sightseer, the effect on the person may at best rival the awe experienced when viewing some magnificent site such as the Grand Canyon. A nice moment that becomes a pleasant memory to be tucked away with the Kodak pictures, but it makes no lasting impact on the way the person lives.

In contrast, when a worshiper is not just observing but is really listening, then worship can be the same kind of change agent that Isaiah experienced. The impact of that divine vision never left him. It was not just a pleasant memory but a life-changing event. Our desire should be to go from worship affected, changed forever.

With performance-based worship, however, where the worshipers are viewed as the audience and the worship leaders and choir as the performers, it is natural for the person in the pew to lapse into the mind-set of a theater critic when the service concludes. In "reviewing" the "performance," a telling comment about the worshiper's attitude is the statement, "I didn't get anything out of it."

But worship is more than a Sunday morning show. We cannot walk away unchanged when in worship we realize who God is and what He has done. What we experience in worship should then affect the way we live—in our homes, in our relationships, in our work, and in our activities. Because we worship God, we put honesty into our business dealings; we carry truthfulness into our conversations; we take love into our relationships; we put witnessing into our words. Worship changes our lives so that we can influence the lives of others.

Making It Real

Real worship transforms lives. When the disciples, after an unsuccessful night of fishing, were told by Jesus to cast their nets into deep water, the result was a catch so large that their nets began to break (Luke 5:3–10). In the presence of this Miracle-Worker, Peter's reaction was not joy over the fish but a realization of his own condition before God. "Go away from me, Lord; I am a sinful man!" (v. 8). The revelation brought a recognition of himself. Peter responded by leaving everything and following Jesus, just as Isaiah before him had done.

To make the transforming effect of worship real in your life:

• Prepare for worship. Expect to hear God's voice. Plan to be moved. Determine to obey.

• Read God's Word, not just to satisfy the requirements of a Bible-reading program but to discover God and yourself. This will not be a mystical, one-time, lightning-strike experience, but an opening of your heart, mind, will, and emotions to God's continuing revelation of Himself.

• Allow God's Spirit to convict you of any sin in your life. As a believer in Christ, you are a forgiven sinner, but you are accountable for living a life of holiness. Be quick to repent—turn around and go in the other direction—then remedy, with God's help, any situation that you have neglected. Remember that worship involves service. "Offer your bodies as living sacrifices . . . this is your reasonable spiritual act of worship," Paul says (Rom. 12:1).

The question we should ask ourselves on the way home from worship is not, "What did I get out of it?" but rather, "How did I do?" How we live reflects the God we worship. A proper approach to worship is not the attitude of "hoping I get something out of this," but the willingness to pray, "Change my heart, O God. Then use me."

GOING DEEPER
(A Personal Study Guide)

Part 1—Getting into the Word

Prayer—The parallels between Isaiah's day and ours are striking. Words written centuries ago still resonate with meaning today because God's eternal Word speaks to all people of all time. Pray that God will give you a fresh look at who He is, who you are in Him, and how you should respond to Him.

Reading/Hearing God's Word—Read Isaiah 6:1–8. Make a list of the words or phrases that describe God. If you skim, you'll miss them. Start with "the LORD," "seated on a throne," and notice the distinction in verse 3 that He is the "LORD." Next to each word or phrase, write the definition. It might take some extra digging, but your search will yield rich nuggets of truth.

_____

_____

_____

_____

Understanding God's Word—Read these verses again. Underline any key phrases or ideas. Then answer the following questions:

1. How is God's holiness emphasized in the words of the angels and Isaiah?

_____

_____

_____

2. How did this vision of God's holiness affect Isaiah?

_____

_____

_____

Meditating on God's Word—Write a paragraph describing your understanding of God's holiness.

_____

_____

_____

Part 2—The Word in Review

Introduction

Isaiah's day was much like ours—a time of prosperity and sinful pride

I. In Worship There Is Revelation: Seeing God As He Is (Isa. 6:1–4)

A. He saw the Lord

B. He heard the praise

II. In Worship There Is Realization: Seeing Ourselves As God Sees Us (6:5–7)

A. He recognized his uncleanness

B. He received cleansing

III. In Worship There Is Response: We Are Changed (6:8)

A. For change to occur, the worshiper must be listening

B. For change to occur, the worshiper must respond

Part 3—Taking the Word into My World

Consider the parallels between Isaiah's day and ours. In what ways do we see pride, prosperity, and a leadership vacuum?

_____

_____

_____

There is an air of uncertainty in a culture dominated by change—change in moral standards, technology, the economy, the work ethic, and family values. What other areas of change would you add to this list?

_____

_____

_____

Sadly, a characteristic of "spirituality" today makes man the center and views God more as a chum or neighbor, someone we drop by to visit on the weekend. Isaiah's view of the Lord was profoundly different—high and exalted. What steps can you take to conform your view of God to Isaiah's?

_____

_____

_____

God is holy. He expects His people to pursue lives of holiness. Think about it. How can a lack of personal holiness affect your worship?

_____

_____

_____

Worship should change us, perhaps not always so dramatically as in Isaiah's experience, but in real and tangible ways. How can our worship affect and change us in the following areas:

1. Our understanding of the holiness of God.

_____

_____

_____

2. Our personal holiness or lack of holiness.

_____

_____

_____

3. What God wants us not only to be but to do.

_____

_____

_____

Part 4—Grabbing Hold

Sometimes it seems we are better at padding the pew than bending the knee. Perhaps the best conclusion to this study is literally time spent on your knees, ascribing praise and adoration to the holy God, confessing your own unworthiness, and offering, as Isaiah did, "Here am I, send me."

CHAPTER 5

WELL ON THE WAY TO WORSHIP

John 4:10–26

"It has been suggested that in worship man needs to intellectualize his emotions and emotionalize his intellect."
—F. Seigler

Midday means two different things to these two Middle-Easterners—one, a traveler on his way to an unknown destination; the other, a village woman involved in one of the daily routines of life. The heat of the day is taking its toll, and the quiet gnawing of hunger suggests a break. Something cool to drink, a bite to eat perhaps, and a bit of rest before traveling on.

The Stranger sits, waiting for the return of His small party of twelve, who have gone to scout out provisions for their meal. It is not the prospect of lunch that interests Him, nor the travel yet ahead. No, it is something far more necessary, far more satisfying. So He waits in the heat of noontime, that point in the day when the shadows stop and time itself seems to linger for an extra long moment. He is waiting for someone, a special someone.

The dust she kicks up as she makes her way along in the glare of the sun reminds her of the wearying dirtiness of her life. Nothing ever removes it completely—that cloying, clinging dirt of her soul—not all the washing in the world.

She puts up a hand to shade her face, shifting the weight of her water pot to the other shoulder. My, but it is hot in this sun! No matter. Better this minor discomfort than the stares, the silence, the snide remarks that destroy self-esteem and scar the spirit. Why go where you are not wanted? So you learn—go to the well when the other women seek the cool of the indoors to attend to their household tasks. She has made this lonely trek many times before.

But today she is not alone. Who is that—there in the distance, sitting on the rim of the well? She approaches hesitantly, until she is close enough to see that the man is a Jew. Most Jews would go miles out of the way to avoid Samaria, home of that most despised of all people.

Suddenly He shatters the silence. "Will you give me a drink?"

The request sounds simple enough. But what does He really want of her? She knows only too well the direction this kind of innocent question can take. He is a Jew; she, a Samaritan. He is a man; she, a woman—a harlot at that and an outcast among her own people. By speaking to her at all, He has ignored the social dictates of the day. Why would He risk His ceremonial cleanness by using a drinking vessel handed to Him by one considered unclean?

She weighs His words carefully as she has often weighed men's words before, tossing them about in her mind as one might jingle coins in the hand, trying to decide if the price is right. Yet there is something different about this man. . . .

As John Piper expresses it so eloquently: "Jesus is bone-weary from the journey. He is hot and thirsty. He decides: 'Yes, even now, just now, I will seek someone to worship the Father—a Samaritan adulteress. I will show my disciples how my Father seeks worship in the midst of real life from the least likely. She is a Samaritan. She is a woman. She is a harlot. Yes, I will even show them a thing or two about how to make true worshippers out of the white harvest of harlots in Samaria.'"[1]

Empty Hearts, Dry Wells (vv. 10–12)

In John 4 is found the most detailed teaching of Jesus in the Bible on the subject of worship. This passage takes us deeper into the issues of the heart, the place from which true worship springs.

Multiple marriages and multiplied relationships have failed to fulfill this woman's deepest needs, leaving her like a dry cistern in the desert. She is desperate, needing to be filled. And now a Jew mocks her, telling her that He can give her "living water" (v. 10).

In a few quick exchanges, uttered without pausing for breath, she attempts to put this Stranger in His place. "You have nothing to draw with and the well is deep. Where can you get this living water? Are you greater than our father Jacob, who gave us the well and drank from it himself, as did also his sons and his flocks and herds?" (vv. 11–12).

As her argument gushes forth like an artesian well, Jesus is willing to wait her out before delivering yet another startling statement: "Go, call your husband and come back" (v. 16).

Now she knows. This is no ordinary man asking for a drink; this, no ordinary day. He must be a prophet, for He knows that she has had five husbands and that the man who is living with her now is not her husband!

It is possible that the woman was simply trying to change the subject with her question about worship. Obviously, this conversation about her personal life could not have been comfortable for her, so she may have chosen to turn it toward the long-standing debate of that day—the proper place to worship God. Samaritans believed that Mount Gerizim was sacred, while the Jews held that Jerusalem was the only place to worship Him.

It is also possible that when she realized that Jesus was a prophet, she was asking not as a diversion but as a seeker. Temporary physical relationships with many men could not fill the jagged hole in her heart. Now a man willing to ignore sexual, religious, and racial prejudices was actually speaking to her in a way that gave her the stirring of hope. Perhaps her deepest need, that of intimacy, could indeed be filled—not by yet another sexual partner, but by God!

Either view is possible. What is certain is this: The discussion that follows draws open the curtain and allows us to view worship as Jesus views it—not as a matter of geographical location, but as a matter of spirit and truth. She asked *where*. He told her *what* worship is and how to become a true worshiper.

True Worship: God's Definition

Out of Jesus' conversation with the Samaritan woman came a profound discovery. "One of the most unexpected aspects in a biblical approach to worship . . . is the fact that God is actively seeking true worshipers."[2]

Jesus' statement in verse 23—"for they are the kind of worshipers *the Father seeks*"—tells us that worship is extremely important to God. It is also important that we understand what God expects of true worshipers. "You Samaritans worship what you do not know" (v. 22). At this time the Bible contained only the Pentateuch, the first five books of the Bible. But it was enough. They "did not know" because they refused to accept all that He had revealed to them in the Scriptures of the Old Testament.

Review time. What is worship? A simple observation on communication is valuable at this point. It has been said that communication is the meeting of meanings. What worship means to one person or group may not be the same for another. As Humpty Dumpty said in the Lewis Carroll classic, *Through the Looking Glass*, "When I use a word . . . it means just what I choose it to mean—neither more nor less."

Or we may consult the wrong source in defining important words. Dictionaries are helpful. But when trying to understand biblical terms, the Bible is our best reference.

The word *worship*, along with such related terms as *worshiper* and *worshiping*, appears more than 250 times in the Bible—approximately 175 times in the Old Testament and 80 times in the New. Although we have touched on this concept in an earlier chapter, the Bible does not use only one Hebrew or Greek word for *worship*, but a variety. You may find that your understanding of worship is narrow and limited when compared to what God's Word has to say.

As we have already mentioned, both the Hebrew and Greek words suggest the idea of "bowing down." Abraham bowed down (*shachah*) to three visitors, one of whom was the Lord Himself (Gen. 18:2). The most frequently used Greek word, *proskuneo*, literally means "to kiss toward, fall down before, kneel, or prostrate oneself in worship." The Magi came "to worship," and when "they saw the child with his mother Mary . . . they bowed down and worshiped him" (Matt. 2:2, 11). Another key Greek word is *latreu*, meaning "to serve," which is translated "worship" in Hebrews 12:28. Both of these words are used much more often in the New Testament.

W. E. Vine points out, "A consideration of the [words translated "worship"] shows that it is not confined to praise; broadly it may be regarded as the direct acknowledgment to God, of His nature, attributes, ways and claims, whether by the outgoing of the heart in praise and thanksgiving or by deeds done in such acknowledgment."[3]

Together, the various words used reveal several aspects of worship.

Worship is reverence. A biblical understanding of worship begins with acknowledging that worship is an attitude of reverence—again, a matter of the heart and not the art. It is a heart of respect, awe, wonder, and fear as we recognize and acknowledge who God is. Two of the words for worship—meaning "to fall down and prostate oneself, to bow or kneel in reverence"—directly refer to a posture that reveals an inner attitude.

If we really saw God as infinitely great, holy, powerful, full of authority and sovereignty, there would be no question about the position of our bodies. When the disciples witnessed the transfiguration, "they fell facedown to the ground, terrified" (Matt. 17:6). John "fell at his feet as though dead" when he saw the Lord (Rev. 1:17). Anne Graham Lotts, daughter of Dr. and Mrs. Billy Graham, once consulted a doctor about knee pain and was told that her prayer life was ruining her knees. Her reply was kind, but firm. "I could not approach my Lord any other way."

Worship is service. Worship is more than attitude. A further study of the words for *worship* reveals that they speak also of actions. We are to serve God. Watching is not serving. Therefore, spending an hour as a spectator does not constitute worship.

Some seem to believe that worship consists of knowing the latest praise songs. Biblical worship is dependent upon knowing and obeying the Word of God. To serve Him means that we do His will, not ours. Knowing what He desires is not necessarily learned through some mystical experience or a voice that speaks in our dreams. God has given us His Word—a practical guide for daily living. Start there! Read the Bible and learn what it teaches. It is here that God clearly tells us about Himself and what He desires of us.

In order to worship God with our actions, there must be a surrender to serve. As we expand our understanding, we will realize that our entire life can be, should be, an act of worship.

Worship is giving offerings to God. One of the first uses of the word *worship* in the Bible is found in Genesis 22—the moving story of Abraham and his son Isaac. "[Abraham] said to his servants, 'Stay here with the donkey while I and the boy go over there. We will worship and then we will come back to you'" (v. 5). The offering Abraham was prepared to make on Mount Moriah was a costly sacrifice—his son.

We declare how much we value something by what we will give for it or to it. In the basic English understanding of the word *worship* is the concept of ascribing worth to something. The worth we ascribe to God is proven by the offerings we are willing to give Him.

Money is only a part of a worthy offering, yet money represents a big part of our lives. When we give of our financial resources, the time, energy, and skills used to generate that income become direct acts of worship. If a person tithes— gives ten percent of all earnings to God—then ten percent of that person's time, energy, and skills is also devoted to Him.

Our giving, though, should include more than finances. Paul rejoiced that the Macedonian churches gave "out of the most severe trial, their overflowing joy and their extreme poverty . . . they gave as much as they were able, and even beyond their ability. . . . they gave themselves first to the Lord" (2 Cor. 8:2–3, 5). In Romans 12:1 Paul describes the offering of our bodies to God as our "spiritual act of worship." It is the Greek word *latreuo*, which means "to serve." We give service as an act of worship.

Worship is praise. Most of us think of music when we use the word *worship*. To sing or play a musical instrument—even when it is for the glory of God—is not just a routine developed to fill the first part of a church service. "Through Jesus, therefore, let us continually offer to God a sacrifice of praise—the fruit of lips that confess his name" (Heb. 13:15).

True worship is singing songs in the night—offering to God our praise when everything around us is dark and uncertain. This is the worship that most pleases Him.

Worship is proclaiming the Gospel to lost souls. Paul said to the Romans: "I have written you quite boldly on some points, as if to remind you of them again, because of the grace God gave me to be a minister of Christ Jesus to the Gentiles with the priestly duty of proclaiming the gospel of God, so that the Gentiles might become an offering acceptable to God, sanctified by the Holy Spirit" (15:15–16). The people we win to Christ are an offering we present to the One who gave Himself for us.

Worship is prayer. In the Book of Revelation, the prayers of the saints are offered before the throne of God. "Another angel, who had a golden censer, came and stood at the altar. He was given much incense to offer, with the prayers of all the saints, on the golden altar before the throne. The smoke of the incense, together with the prayers of the saints, went up before God" (8:3–4).

Every prayer we pray, if offered in sincerity, is stored for the time of fulfillment. The answer may not be the expected outcome, but God does not take lightly the soul's sincere desire.

The giving of our finances, our service, the fruit of our

witness, our praise, and our fervent prayers are all acts of worship. We respond to God and declare His worth through the gifts we bring.

Responding to God

I have referenced Warren Wiersbe several times, but his treatment of worship bears repeating. His book *Real Worship*, which has been expanded and revised, is one of the finest works available on the subject. After considering biblical terms, definitions by others, and both the objective and subjective aspects to worship, he states, "No definition is final, so accept this one for the time being. . . . Worship is the believers' response of all that they are—mind, emotions, will, and body—to what God is and says and does. This response has its mystical side in subjective experience and its practical side in objective obedience to God's revealed will. Worship is a loving response that's balanced by the fear of the Lord, and it is a deepening response as the believer comes to know God better."[4]

The key word is *response*. In true worship, all that we are responds to all that God is and says and does. Our lives are to be lived in response to Him. Worship is active, not passive; continuous, not intermittent; the totality of our lives and being, not the partiality of our existence.

God is looking for worshipers, people whose response to Him results in changed attitudes and actions and a change in the way we give to Him. A life of worship will include times of regular corporate worship as well as intimate quiet times of personal worship. All of reality is affected by the way we regard God. Our attitudes, actions, and offerings will flow out of hearts that have been transformed.

God is to be the only Object of our worship. Not only is the worship of other gods forbidden in the Decalogue, but Jesus reprimanded the Tempter: "Away from me, Satan! For it is written: 'Worship the Lord your God, and serve him only'" (Matt. 4:10). To the Samaritan woman, He said, "Believe me, woman, a time is coming when you will worship the Father neither on this mountain nor in Jerusalem. . . . Yet a time is coming and has now come when the true worshipers will worship the Father in spirit and truth" (John 4:21, 23). While these verses mention the place of worship as well as the balance of worship—"spirit and truth"—both point to God as the central figure. God will not share worship. It is to be directed to Him alone.

Since God is Spirit, we must worship Him in spirit. He cannot be reduced to an image. His instructions are clear: "You shall not make for yourself an idol in the form of anything in heaven above or on the earth beneath or in the waters below" (Ex. 20:4).

Nor can the worship of God be confined to a place. This strikes at the original question of the woman at the well. It is not a matter of going to Mount Gerizim or Mount Moriah, Calvary Baptist or Christ Community. It is a matter of the state of the heart.

It was a woman, an outcast among her own people, who was first in her village to ask, "Could this man be the Christ?" (4:29). She recognized Him as the Savior. She received Him as the Deliverer from a lifestyle of wantonness to a lifestyle of worship. After one conversation, her heart stirred with worship made real.

Making It Real

Like the woman at the well, every person has a need for intimacy that can be met in our relationship with God. Sometimes He allows pain, rejection, or disillusionment to bring us to our knees. This woman had sought peace and contentment in temporary sexual relationships with men who used her and left her empty and unfulfilled. But nothing she tried filled the aching hole in her heart. It was Jesus who offered living water—by filling her cup with Him, she would never thirst again.

When you are ready to tap into the Living Water, you will find that true worship is as natural as breathing and that there is only One who is worthy to receive your reverence, your service, and your offerings of prayer, praise, proclamation, and finances.

Begin now to believe what Jesus told that thirsty woman:

• Worship is not confined to a time or place. This is not an excuse to skip corporate worship or to beg off being a part of a local church. It does, however, make worship always possible wherever you are, whatever your circumstances.

• Worship is acknowledging that you are unclean but that God can cleanse you. That unworthy woman didn't have a clue that day that she would meet a Man who was more interested in cleaning up the inside than what was on the outside.

• Worship is meeting God at the point of your need to receive all He has for you and to give all you have to Him. What an exchange! But that's what happens in a divine encounter, in a moment of true worship.

When was the last time you were staggered by the revelation of who God really is? Once that happens, you won't need seminars, the hottest book on the subject, the latest tape series — you'll be well on your way to worship!

GOING DEEPER
(A Personal Study Guide)

Part 1—Getting into the Word

Prayer—In this passage we find Jesus' most comprehensive statement on worship. Ask God to help you grasp that worship is not a musical performance, but involves attitudes, actions, and offerings.

Reading/Hearing God's Word—Read or listen to John 4:1–42. Don't shortchange your study by skipping this long passage! One way to slow down and really absorb the meaning is to read it aloud, in more than one translation (*King James Version, New King James Version, New American Standard Bible*, or *New International Version*). Some paraphrases might give a fresh look at the verses, but remember that they are not translations. Study a reliable translation first, using paraphrases only as a supplement.

Understanding God's Word—Read the verses again. Underline any key phrases or ideas. Then answer the following questions:

1. Do you think the woman was trying to change the subject, or did she really want to know more about worship?

_____

_____

_____

2. What are the important things Jesus said about worship?

_____

_____

_____

Meditating on God's Word—Write a brief summary of a meaningful verse or idea.

_____

_____

_____

73

Part 2—The Word in Review

Introduction

The story of the woman at the well retold

I. Empty Hearts, Dry Wells (John 4:1–16)

A. Temporary, physical relationships do not meet the needs of a soul

B. God offers what truly satisfies

II. True Worship: God's Definition (4:17–26)

A. Worship is reverence

B. Worship is service

C. Worship is giving offerings to God

1. Finances

2. Ourselves

3. Praise

4. People won to Christ

5. Prayer

Summary: Worship involves our attitude, actions, and offerings

III. Responding to God

A. Key word is *response*

B. God is Spirit, not an image or a place

Part 3—Taking the Word into My World

It was not by coincidence that Jesus chose a woman with an immoral lifestyle with whom to discuss spiritual matters. Learning to worship—in spirit and in truth—will bring about change in any life, no matter how deep the sin!

Consider again this paragraph: "Like the woman at the well, every person has a need for intimacy that can be met in our relationship with God. Sometimes He allows pain, rejection, or disillusionment to bring us to our knees. This woman had sought peace and contentment in temporary sexual relationships with men who used her and left her empty and unfulfilled. But nothing she tried filled the aching hole in her heart. It was Jesus who offered living water—by filling her cup with Him, she would never thirst again.

Some still confine worship to a time, a place, or a specific form. Why does that type of worship fail to meet the deepest needs of our lives?

_____

_____

_____

How can we adjust our worship in the following areas:

1. Attitudes _____

2. Actions _____

3. Offerings _____

Part 4—Grabbing Hold

It may help to memorize, or at least write on an index card, Warren Wiersbe's definition of *worship*. Use as a memory jogger the words *attitudes, actions*, and *offerings*.

Continue to assess your heart. Where do you stand in regard to these three areas? Perhaps you have unintentionally confined worship to a place, time, or particular format. Relinquish all rights to your own worship agenda and determine to learn and follow God's definition.

CHAPTER 6

WORSHIP: A WORK IN PROGRESS

Nehemiah 1

"Worship is the test of the authenticity of any conversion, whether to Christianity or some other religion. But the factor that distinguishes our faith from every other creed is the intimacy of our relationship with the living God."
—Tom Inglis

Wander into a music store. Examine the gleaming new instruments. It might be an acoustic guitar, a lyric flute, or a cello that catches your eye. Pick out a shiny brass trumpet. You love the sounds it makes when the notes soar, mellow and golden, valves flying as the music ascends and descends the scale with almost dizzying speed.

Now you are going to make that cold piece of metal sing with the warmth of melody. You walk out of that store, instrument case in hand, anticipating the enjoyment ahead when the musician in you can express itself.

Once a week, open the case. Take the instrument in your hands, dreaming of the music you know it is capable of producing. Place your fingers on the valves as you grip the horn in your hands, bring it to your lips, and blow.

What was that sound? Probably not like anything you've ever heard before! Definitely not like the CDs you enjoy. Still, give it a good try and then, after a few more discordant noises, put it away.

A week later, take the trumpet out of the case again. The wonderful new smell still greets your senses as the lid is opened. What a beauty! No dents or scratches, only the potential of making glorious music. You love this horn, want to protect it, want to play it. So you put the mouthpiece to your lips again and . . . same sad sound as last week. Maybe next time.

On a weekly basis you repeat this ritual. But it's no use. Why bother? The sound in your heart is not the one in your ear. You're tempted to quit, give up, get your money back.

So, what's the problem? Probably nothing that a few lessons and some hours of practice couldn't fix. Good musicianship takes work!

◆

It's Sunday. You resist the urge to roll over and sleep in. You make it to the church in time to greet some old friends. It is enjoyable to be here in this place where you anticipate the experience of God's presence in a special way. The service begins and you realize that here, in this room, other people are connecting with God. You can tell from the joyous expressions on their faces.

But it isn't happening for you. Maybe it was the baby crying, or the interruption to announce that someone had left their headlights on in the parking lot. Maybe next week.

Seven days later, like a bright, shiny trumpet taken from its case, you hold before you the time of corporate worship. And just like those unsuccessful attempts to play the horn produced disappointment, so your worship experience continues to be unfulfilling. Maybe this is the way it will always be.

So, what's the problem? Many people, having never been taught much about worship, experience an inability to interact with God on a deeper level. They find themselves following well-worn paths, sensing that there is more that continues to elude them. Real worship takes work.

Any relationship worth having and keeping requires nurturing. That is true with a spouse, a best friend, a family member—and with God. It is in the Book of Nehemiah that we find a model to help us work at our worship.

Rebuilding Our Worship (v. 3)

When we think of Nehemiah, we generally think of the

man who rebuilt the wall of Jerusalem after the Babylonian assault and captivity. But this book is not about a man. It is a book about God. From the opening scene, it is God who commands center stage.

It is God to whom Nehemiah turns when he hears about the devastation of Jerusalem—that the wall of the city has been "broken down, and its gates have been burned" (1:3). It is God who hears Nehemiah's broken-hearted prayer, gives him favor with a pagan king, and leads him to attempt the rebuilding.

Then in Jerusalem, as the work is opposed, Nehemiah answers his critics: "The God of heaven will give us success" (2:20). The builders, who work with tools in one hand and weapons in the other, are further encouraged: "Our God will fight for us!" (4:20). God is the Helper upon whom Nehemiah calls and the One to whom he commits his enemies. And when the work is completed, even those enemies "realized that this work had been done with the help of . . . God" (6:16).

The building program concluded with a worship service by the people who had experienced the blessing of God in their midst. Yet this service was not a one-hour or even a one-day event; interaction with God had been going on since the beginning of reconstruction. And it all began with a prayer—a prayer that gives us much insight into the character of Nehemiah and provides a model for personal worship.

Worship: One-On-One (vv. 4–11)

First reactions reveal a lot about a person. When informed about the sorry state of Jerusalem by his brother Hanani, what did Nehemiah do? Rant and rave? Threaten retaliation against his enemies? Blame God? Give up in despair? No, he "sat down and wept. . . . [He] mourned and fasted and prayed before the God of heaven" (v. 4).

A sense of awe. Practically every phrase of this prayer tells us that Nehemiah was a man of humility, acknowledging "'the great and awesome God, who keeps his covenant of love with whose who love him and obey his commands'" (v. 5).

Nehemiah was in awe—not scared to death, but properly reverent toward a loving and just Sovereign. To him, the Lord God was worthy of praise.

The Bible's capitalized spelling of LORD indicates that this is the Hebrew name *Yahweh*, the redemptive name of God, described as the "God of heaven." This is the Supreme and Sovereign Creator of the universe, and Nehemiah recognized His "worth-ship."

When I began my ministry to professional baseball players, I was in awe of the locker room. Over the door was a sign reading, "No Admittance," but since I was the team chaplain, I was allowed to enter. Often people gathered outside that door, hoping for an autograph and watching in wonder as I walked by, confidently and nonchalantly opened the door, and disappeared from sight. Whenever someone accompanied me into the locker room—their first time to mingle with the pros—I was reminded of the sense of awe that I had lost. It had become routine for me and the thrill was gone, but their wide eyes brought it all back.

In a culture where casual is in, it's easy to lose our sense of awe. When we want to make worship real, we must renew our sense of the awesomeness of God. Read carefully the passages that describe His majesty: Job 38–42:6; Isaiah 6, 40; Revelation 4–5. Notice how people responded to God's messengers, to His message. Ask Him to reveal Himself in all His beauty and glory—in a sunset, in the flashing crash of a thunderbolt, or the soft, silent descent of a snowflake.

When Nehemiah began to pray, it was not to plead for God's blessing but to acknowledge who and what God is. Remember that the meaning of *worship* includes "responding to all that God is and says and does." In responding, Nehemiah was taking the first step toward authentic worship.

Confessing our sins. A significant aspect of Nehemiah's prayer is his confession. "I confess the sins we Israelites, including myself and my father's house, have committed against you. We have acted very wickedly toward you. We have not obeyed the commands, decrees and laws you gave your servant Moses" (vv. 6–7). No skirting the issue. No copping out. Simply a straightforward admission of the facts.

Nehemiah didn't sidestep his share of the blame either. He included himself in that list of sinners.

These wicked acts were an affront to God Himself, and the people had no excuse. Through Moses, God had given them the commands, decrees, and laws that would enable them to lead peaceful, productive lives. But they wouldn't listen, a fact that resulted in dire consequences. Nehemiah's change of address was proof. The captivity of Israel was a direct judgment of God on the sins of His people.

The words of Isaiah the prophet are as true in our day as they were in his: "The Lord, the LORD Almighty, called you on that day to weep and to wail, to tear out your hair and put on sackcloth. But see, there is joy and revelry, slaughtering of cattle and killing of sheep, eating of meat and drinking of wine! 'Let us eat and drink,' you say, 'for tomorrow we die'" (22:12–13). The people would not let God's call to repentance disturb their party.

But Nehemiah's was another story. Undoubtedly it was his example of confession that stirred others to follow. At Ezra's reading of the law, the people spent a quarter of the day listening and another quarter "in confession and in worshiping the LORD their God" (9:3). Confession is linked to worship. The bulk of the chapter is their prayer of confession, one that was recorded, made into a binding agreement, then signed and sealed by the leaders.

The worship of God is inseparably linked to the purity of our hearts. The priestly garments described in the Old Testament included a gold plate, engraved like an inscription on a seal: "HOLY TO THE LORD" (Ex. 39:30). It was a visible reminder of the importance of holiness as the priest carried out the work of ministry. Before Moses and Aaron entered the Tent of Meeting, sacrifices were offered (Lev. 9). Of utmost importance was the purification of that priest before entering into the presence of God. Leviticus 16 tells of the sacrifices and cleansing that were to take place on that day.

Without confession, there is no cleansing. While sin remains in our lives, our relationship with God cannot deepen. John wrote of those who "walk in darkness" yet "claim to have fellowship with him" (1 John 1:6). Fellowship is dependent upon walking in the light and being purified from all sin. That purification is no longer dependent upon the priestly sacrifices, since the Lamb of God came to offer Himself as the only remaining sacrifice. Now we can receive daily cleansing as we worship. "If we confess our sins, he is faithful and just and will forgive us our sins and purify us from all unrighteousness" (v. 9).

To become a true worshiper, confession is not an option but a requirement. As you look at this model of Nehemiah's devotional life, consider your own. I hope you share his view of sin. If so, you will let the Lord clean up your act so you may enter into His presence.

Knowing the Word of God. Nehemiah was a man of the Word. "Remember the instruction you gave your servant Moses, saying . . . ," he prayed (v. 8). Catch the implication here. Nehemiah must have studied God's Word in order to know it well and be able to use it so effectively in his prayer life.

To worship God we must know Him. That's not so difficult. He is not hiding from us; He reveals Himself to us in His Word. He gives us instructions on what is acceptable and unacceptable in worship.

The psalmist's appreciation for the Word of God was such that he considered it to be like the taste of honey: "How sweet are your words to my taste, sweeter than honey to my mouth!" (Ps. 119:103). On the other hand, there are times when God's Word is anything but sweet; rather, more like a sword that pierces our hearts: "The word of God is living and active. Sharper than any double-edged sword, it penetrates even to dividing soul and spirit, joints and marrow; it judges the thoughts and attitudes of the heart" (Heb. 4:12).

Yet another imagery is used by the prophet Jeremiah: "But if I say, 'I will not mention him or speak any more in his name,' his word is in my heart like a burning fire, a fire shut up in my bones. I am weary of holding it in; indeed, I cannot" (Jer. 20:9). God's Word, like a consuming fire, cannot be contained. It spills forth in proclamation, in prophecy . . . and in worship.

These poetic images are powerful, but for the Word to affect our worship, it must be brought into the reality of our lives. God did not give us His Word just to increase our knowledge but to affect the way we live. We need a faith that goes beyond the church parking lot, one that is carried into our day-to-day existence, that affects our relationships with people, and is seen in our words and deeds.

Serious worship arises from serious Bible reading—not the skim-it, scan-it, mark-off-another-day kind of reading. Once, while driving with my wife, I came to a stop sign, made the stop, then proceeded on without really noticing what the sign said. When Joan asked me if I had read the sign, I admitted I had not. I was so accustomed to the octagonal red shape that I had not seen these additional words on the sign, "Look again." Perhaps we need a bookmark for our Bibles labeled, "Look again!" We need to read our Bibles— mind in gear.

Ask God to give you a passion for His Word, then try reading Psalm 119. Don't balk at the fact that this is the longest psalm in the Bible; it is a great place to begin. Each section begins with a letter in the Hebrew alphabet—*aleph, beth, gimel,* and so on. The first word in the line of a stanza begins with the same letter. Almost every verse mentions the Word of God. Read slowly, marking each reference to the Word, looking for the synonyms: *law, statutes, precepts, decrees,* and *commands.*

The next time through, read verses 1–8 only—the first stanza—searching for what the psalmist says about the Word of God. The psalm begins by declaring that those who walk according to the law of the Lord will be blessed. Ask God to help you have the same heart attitude as the psalmist.

Each day read the next segment, looking for another nugget of truth. As you pray that truth into your own life,

God will hear your prayer, give you a hunger and thirst for His Word, and bring new life to your worship.

Learning to pray "successfully." The last part of Nehemiah's worship model is a renewed thrust of prayer. His request quite simply is, "Give your servant success today by granting him favor" (v. 11). We hear from God through His Word; He hears from us in our prayers.

Nehemiah's prayer life challenges us to strive for excellence. He prayed for extended periods of time, repeatedly, spontaneously, and persistently—and God answered. Nehemiah was a man of prayer, and if we are hoping to advance our relationship with God, we will do well to follow his example.

Our devotional life can be helped along by a prayer list. Just as we may have a grocery list, a to-do list, or even a wish list, a prayer list will serve to remind us of the events, people, and needs for which we should pray.

In his book *A Call to Spiritual Reformation*, D. A. Carson outlines a workable plan for prayer.[1] All it takes is a manila folder and some paper. Head each sheet of paper with a different category. The first should be the people you want to remember on a regular basis—family, church members, and close friends.

The second category is short-range or intermediate-range concerns. These include people and situations for which you will be praying on a temporary basis—illnesses, ministry events, and current situations. Add pages as needed.

The rest of the folder will be filled with letters and prayer cards filed in alphabetical order. When a new letter or e-mail comes from a missionary or friend, highlight the requests and then replace the one currently in the folder. As you have time to pray for these requests, start with the letter on top. After you have prayed for that one, place it on the bottom of the stack. In time, it will rotate to the top again. This plan will help to make us people of prayer.

It has been said that we work at our play, play at our

worship, and worship our work. We need to work at our worship. The result will be worship that is real.

Making It Real

Our quest to worship the living God begins with a commitment. We must decide that we want to grow in our relationship with Him. In their most basic form, the first steps in this process are to acknowledge God's sovereignty, confess sins, grow in the knowledge of the Word of God, and learn to pray effectively.

Here are some other suggestions that should add depth and meaning to worship, One-on-one:

• Read books that will inspire and instruct you in deepening your relationship with God, such as *Pursuit of Holiness*, by A. W. Tozer, *Desiring God*, by John Piper, *Spiritual Disciplines for the Christian Life*, by Donald S. Whitney, and *Fresh Wind, Fresh Fire* and *Fresh Power*, both by Jim Cymbala.

• Add Bible memorization to your list of spiritual disciplines. Memorizing Bible verses does not have to end with Vacation Bible School. Adults, too, can still commit to memory the precious truths of God's Word.

• Learn how to keep a journal. Taking time to record what God is doing in your life will bring new vitality to your quiet times. Causes for praise will not be easily forgotten, defeats will be remembered so as not to be repeated, and vows and decisions will not be neglected.

• Commit to times of fasting—from the media, from food, from certain kinds of activities—to sharpen your ability to hear God.

• Evaluate your time in the car. The average work commute is thirty minutes. You can choose to fill your time with noise or listen to programming that is uplifting. If Christian radio broadcasting is not available where you live, try Bible-reading and -teaching cassettes during your drive time. Or exercise the option of silence. Your *commuting* could become a time for *communing*.

• Use a variety of music in your personal time with God. Try Scripture set to music, instrumental meditation tapes, and other songs that edify, not simply entertain.

Now we are getting to the crux of the matter—developing the kind of heart God desires. That heart beats for the things of God. It is a heart that is fired up and focused, resulting in worship that doesn't stop with intellectual exercise but changes lives. It is a heart like His. Read on.

GOING DEEPER
(A Personal Study Guide)

Part 1—Getting into the Word

Prayer—As you begin this study, pray the prayer of Nehemiah to prepare your heart for worship work:

> "O LORD, God of heaven, the great and awesome God, who keeps his covenant of love with those who love him and obey his commands, let your ear be attentive and your eyes open to hear the prayer your servant is praying before you day and night for your servants, the people of Israel [your family/your church]. I confess the sins we Israelites, including myself and my father's house, have committed against you. We have acted very wickedly toward you. We have not obeyed the commands, decrees, and laws you gave your servant Moses. . . .
>
> "O Lord, let your ear be attentive to the prayer of this your servant and to the prayer of your servants who delight in revering your name. Give your servant success today by granting him favor" (1:5–7, 11).

Reading/Hearing God's Word—Read or listen to Nehemiah 1. Watch for verses or ideas that strike a responsive chord today. Notice how Nehemiah's time of worship was inspired by a real-life episode, much like Job's experience. Bad news drove both men to their knees.

Understanding God's Word—Read this chapter again. Underline any key phrases or ideas that seem especially meaningful to you. Then look back through these verses and answer the following questions:

1. Why did Hanani's statement in verse 3 affect Nehemiah so drastically?

_____

_____

_____

2. Verse 4 mentions five action steps Nehemiah took. List them here:

    a. _____

    b. _____

    c. _____

    d. _____

    e. _____

3. What is fasting? (This is a question that may require additional study!)

_____

_____

_____

Meditating on God's Word—Write a brief summary of a meaningful verse or idea you noticed.

_____

_____

_____

Why did you choose this particular verse? Is there a specific way in which it applies to your life today?

_____

_____

_____

Part 2—The Word in Review

Introduction

> Imagine worship being like a musical instrument taken out of its case weekly.

I. Rebuilding Our Worship (Neh. 1:3)

> Just as the walls of Jerusalem needed to be rebuilt after the devastation of the enemy assault, so our worship needs times of refreshing.

II. Worship: One-On-One (1:4–11)

> A. A sense of awe
> B. Confessing our sins
> C. Knowing the Word of God
> D. Learning to pray successfully

Part 3—Taking the Word into My World

The opening illustration in this chapter vividly portrays the reason some people do not feel "connected" with God in worship at church. The model is one that can be applied specifically to our lives as we develop the heart God desires.

Go over the words that indicate Nehemiah's sense of awe. What other biblical passages can you find in which the writer communicates a similar attitude toward God? For example, read Isaiah 40:12–31 and list the phrases that are "awesome" statements about Him.

_____

_____

_____

A little tougher assignment is to find other references in the Old Testament—some that are the basis for Nehemiah's prayer. Look for passages where God promised to scatter the people and ultimately gather them again.

What request did Nehemiah bring to God? Do not just write down his words, but explain them.

_____

_____

_____

Read 1 John 1, noticing what John writes about both acknowledging sin and confessing it. Compare what he says to what Nehemiah did.

_____

_____

_____

Part 4—Grabbing Hold

Take each of the four basic parts of this lesson and use them to measure your devotional life.

1. **A sense of awe**. Are you aware that we serve an awesome God? How would you rate your attitude toward His magnificence?

_____

_____

_____

2. **Confession**. Do you have a heart of repentance? Is your conscience soft and sensitive to the Spirit's nudges when you've gone down the wrong path? Is there evidence of change in your life?

_____

_____

_____

3. **Knowing the Word**. What is your pattern of reading the Word of God? Do you make this a regular part of your day, a spiritual discipline that is consistently practiced? A helpful resource is the devotional book *FaithWalk*, which is available

from Back to the Bible. It guides you through reading the Bible in a year, one day at a time.

_____

_____

_____

4. **Prayer**. How do you keep track of prayer requests, and how faithfully do you intercede for others?

_____

_____

_____

Grab hold of the resources available for rebuilding your worship, then resolve to follow through. Celebrate successes with praise and worship, giving all the glory to God!

CHAPTER 7

THE HOLY BALANCE: HEART AND HEAD

Psalm 95, John 4:23–24

"Worship is one of those activities every sincere Christian knows he ought to be doing, and even wants to do. But we're not always sure how to go about it. Like the puzzled party-goers who ask, 'Are we having fun yet?' Christians sometimes try hard to worship, but feel like asking, 'Are we worshiping yet'?"
—Tony Evans

"Get fired up!"

"Stay focused!"

"Put your heart into it!"

"Use your head!"

A locker-room challenge from the coach? Could be. In the heat of athletic competition, any or all of these comments could be made. Or this might be self-talk, phrases used by players to motivate themselves to do their best. To stay in the game, it takes both head and heart—knowledge of the sport and a desire to win. Balance.

The same is true of worship. In worship, there is need for both reason and emotion. As someone has wisely said, "The most important eighteen inches is the distance from the head to the heart." Think of the ball players who really "know" the game but don't have the heart for it anymore. They'll talk about "hanging up the spikes" because they are no longer "having fun." It is not a knowledge problem, but a heart problem.

Then there is the person whose enthusiasm is sky-high but who doesn't have a clue about how to play the game. What about the first-year Little Leaguer, thrilled with the new uniform, the glove with the facsimile signature of a Major League player, darting to right field? Right field—that netherworld of baseball for those young players of high enthusiasm but low skill. As you probably know, rarely does a batter at that level of competition hit a ball to right field! In worship, as in athletics, we need to strive for balance. A holy balance.

Jack Hayford, in his book *Worship His Majesty*, explains the dilemma well: "We are at a great watershed point of Christian worship—and fellowship. There are strong opinions, deep emotions and intense boundary lines drawn on this theme. . . . Every believer possesses the wisdom to recognize that worship is not a single-dimensional exercise of the human personality. Worship is certainly not a cerebral pursuit, some sort of mystical consciousness or an emotional binge, although it does involve reason, spiritual intuition and emotions. Worship . . . involves the total human being—spirit, mind, emotions, and body."[1] It's a matter of the holy balance.

Yet as worshipers, we tend to gravitate toward what feels comfortable. Which is it for you? Shouts to the Lord? Silence? Hand clapping? Knee bending? If you are the intense type, you may struggle with times of quiet contemplation. If you thrive on objective truth, you may suppress emotion because of a real or perceived danger of basing belief on feeling. Each of these extremes has the potential to clash rather than to complement, like a pipe organ and a drum duet.

Envision a service in the church you attend. Perhaps the music is sung from a hymnal, or the words may be projected onto a screen. If your services are liturgical in nature, the image in your mind may be that of responsive readings, a split chancel, and a robed pastor at the front. Or your church may meet in a gym, with chairs and equipment set up each Sunday morning, only to be packed away afterward.

On any given Sunday, you can find a church that uses only a piano and organ. Nothing else is allowed. In a church that meets down the street, a drummer sits behind a Plexiglas wall to control the volume, and the platform is decorated with speakers, amplifiers, wires, instruments and music stands—perhaps even a lectern, all but invisible, since it, too, is Plexiglas. Taped accompaniment may be utilized or vilified, depending on the musical stance of the church leaders. And these are only some of the contrasts we find here in the United States.

Move to a location overseas, and the varieties of worship styles are seemingly endless. Worship with a tribal group in the upper Amazon will not be like a service at an inner-city church. The practices of believers who live in an Islamic country may be in sharp contrast to praise gatherings in America. It has been my privilege to worship in such diverse places as Haiti, Bangladesh, Peru, Jamaica, and Pennsylvania, to hear songs sung to God that reflect the music of each culture. And while perhaps not recognizing a word that was sung, I could tell that they were songs of praise. It was not the *substance* of worship but the *style* that varied.

Yes, as worshipers our tendency may be to opt for the familiar, to go with what feels comfortable. So maybe it's time to get back to the Bible for a course correction. Wouldn't it be more appropriate to ask God—the object of our praise—what kind of worship He prefers?

David, the shepherd psalmist, was a man after God's own heart. In his collection of songs—the ancient hymnal of the second temple—he demonstrates the balance of worship that God loves. Psalm 95 might have been inspired by an assembly like this. . . .

A Balance of Emotion (Ps. 95:1–6)

For some gathered outside the temple courts in Jerusalem, it was difficult to contain their excitement. From outlying areas of the region, they had come to join the crowd for worship. Just the sight of that magnificent structure was enough to kindle their fervor to a fever pitch. Some of them stood on tiptoe, straining to see the priest who was preparing to address the throng.

For others, the event was just another day in the life of a temple worshiper. The only bother was all those country bumpkins with their noisy clamoring. So unseemly. Such utter disregard for proper decorum. Why, they had been known to break out in embarrassing emotional displays. Didn't they know that the temple represented God's presence among His people? Someone really ought to tell them that their conduct was hardly worthy of the Almighty. Perhaps today the priest would say something about curbing these ridiculous outbursts.

The summons to praise is issued. "Come, let us sing for joy to the LORD; let us shout aloud to the Rock of our salvation. . . . Come, let us bow down in worship; let us kneel before the Lord our Maker" (Ps. 95:1, 6).

Well, which is it? Celebration or contemplation? Joyful shouts just don't blend with bended knees, do they? Apparently, God has a difference of opinion.

Worship in Old Testament times was often vigorous and demonstrative. At other times, it was quiet, calm, conducted in an atmosphere of hushed awe. In biblical worship there is a holy balance—both reverent celebration and reverent contemplation. God is pleased with a variety of styles—as long as the heart is sincere.

Get fired up! Verses 1–5 of Psalm 95 are a call to worship with enthusiasm and exuberance: "Sing for joy," "shout aloud," "extol him with music and song." A celebration is to be held in honor of the great God, the King of kings!

As we read the worship scenes of the Bible, we find frequent references to celebration. David was seen "leaping and dancing before the LORD" (2 Sam. 6:16) with such exhilaration that his wife described his actions as being those of a vulgar person. "I will celebrate before the LORD," David insisted (v. 21). When the wall was dedicated in Jerusalem, "the sound of rejoicing . . . could be heard far away" (Neh. 12:43). Repeatedly the Word of God exhorts us to celebrate Him.

Stay focused! The tone of the psalm shifts, suddenly and dramatically, as we are encouraged to worship with reverent contemplation. "Come, let us bow down in worship" (v. 6). We are exhorted to be still, to incline our heads, to reflect on the beauty of His holiness.

When the glory of the Lord filled the temple and the priests could not enter because of it, when the Israelites saw the fire coming down, the Bible records that the people "knelt on the pavement with their faces to the ground, and they worshiped and gave thanks to the LORD, saying, 'He is good; his love endures forever'" (2 Chron. 7:3). Isaiah saw seraphim—angels with three pairs of wings, who burned with zeal for the holiness of God—"calling to one another: 'Holy, holy, holy is the LORD Almighty; the whole earth is full of his glory'" (Isa. 6:3). Yes, we celebrate, but there are also to be times of worshipful meditation.

There is an interesting balance in this psalm. Like the song it is, the melody line carries the constant theme of worshiping God. Providing the harmony are contrasting chords of celebration and contemplation, both in the same piece. These may seem contradictory, but they are really complementary and lend variety to the score—and to the worship.

Some practice a style of worship that is subdued and somber. No talking during the prelude, please! Others, proverbially speaking, "swing from the chandeliers." Warren Wiersbe writes, "It's unfortunate that we often minimize the importance of feelings in our experience of worship. We preach about presenting our bodies as a living sacrifice (Rom. 12:1–2), but then we want to anesthetize our nervous system and eliminate normal emotional response. Our churches are filled with icy people like Michal, David's wife, who criticized her husband because he was too fervent in his worship (2 Sam. 6:20). While we certainly want to avoid shallow emotionalism, we dare not grieve the Holy Spirit in our desire to be 'proper'."[2]

Whichever style of worship, whatever form it takes, there must be the proper attitude. When we, His creatures, enter the presence of the Creator, we must do so with reverence.

A Balance of Content (John 4:23–24)

While we are working through style issues, we may miss two elements that Jesus Himself called "musts." Not once but twice, in consecutive verses, Jesus says that true worshipers must worship in spirit and in truth (vv. 23–24).

The order in which these words are found in the Greek give added emphasis to their importance. "In spirit and in truth" is moved forward, in front of the verb "to worship." In the original language, the verse literally reads, "in spirit and in truth it is necessary to worship." That is the equivalent of putting the phrase in bold-face type.

Put your heart into it! The "spirit" referred to in these verses in John is not the Holy Spirit, although the Holy Spirit does help us in our worship (Rom. 8:26–27). There is no definite article in the Greek to warrant translating the verse with that interpretation—"in the (Holy) Spirit."

When Jesus says that we are to worship "in spirit," He is speaking of the human spirit, the inner person. He is affirming the fact that true worship involves the emotions. One can be in the right place at the right time, wear the right clothing, say the right prayers, sing the right songs, stand and sit at the right time—and still not worship, because worship is not a matter of what happens on the outside but of what flows from the inside. Worship springs from the spirit. Worship is outward—at times it will be visible in what is said and done—but it must begin in the heart.

Verse 24 is also stating that worship must contain that which conforms to the divine nature of God, the Father, whom we are to worship as spirit. It must also conform to the nature of God, who is Himself the embodiment of truth.

In addition, this passage from John gives us an interesting contrast. The controversy raised by the Samaritan woman centered on where to worship—Mount Gerizim or Mount Moriah. Gerizim was the seat of Samaritan worship. The Samaritans rejected all of the Old Testament except their own version of the Pentateuch; their knowledge of God was deficient. The worship that occurred on Mount Gerizim was described by some as enthusiastic heresy; it had spirit but not truth.

In contrast, the worship in Jerusalem at Mount Moriah was barren, lifeless orthodoxy. Jerusalem had the truth, but not the spirit. Jesus rebuked both styles of worship when He said, "God is spirit, and his worshipers must worship in spirit and in truth" (v. 24). Worship is not found at the extremes, but in a balance of content.

The Samaritan woman was asking the wrong question. Worship is never a matter of place or time. Worship operates not in the sphere of the material world, but in the spiritual — and any worship that is reduced to time and place is not biblical worship.

Worship is not only what we think, it is also what we feel. It is not just an acknowledgment, but a response. One without the other is only half the equation.

Use your head! When Jesus tells us to worship "in truth," He draws our attention to the centrality of truth. The immediate implication of truth in worship is that it is the opposite of falsehood. What is said, sung, taught, done must be in agreement with the truth of God. His truth, in John's Gospel, is associated with Christ Himself, who said, "I am the way and the truth and the life" (14:6), and who is described as being "full of grace and truth" (1:14).

To worship in truth, we are driven to the Word of God (17:17). We need to know the Word in order to determine if we are true worshipers. The truth God requires is not our version, but worship that is grounded on, based upon, in agreement with, and an expression of His truth.

"Worship is not an emotional exercise with God-words that induce certain feelings. Worship is a response built upon truth," writes John MacArthur in his book *The Ultimate Priority*.[3] A person may know the words of the worship songs, but be ignorant of the Word from which they come. This person may experience all kinds of "warm fuzzies," but lack knowledge. For our worship to be biblical, there must be both emotion and truth.

John Piper warns: "Truth without emotion produces dead orthodoxy and a church full (or half-full) of artificial admirers. . . . On the other hand, emotion without truth produces empty frenzy and cultivates shallow people who refuse the discipline of rigorous thought. But true worship comes from people who are deeply emotional and who love deep and sound doctrine. Strong affections for God rooted in truth are the bone and marrow of biblical worship."[4]

Jesus presents a balanced picture of worship. Where do you need to adjust your thinking and behavior? Are you all celebration or all contemplation? Are you all emotion or all objective truth? We must not worship at Mount Gerizim or Mount Moriah, but in the heart of the Father.

Making It Real

Balance in worship is not just a matter of preference; it should be a priority. In the Old Testament, David discovered the heart of worship; Jesus personified it in the New. It's all there—in the Book! A careful reading of the Word reveals that there is to be balance in the areas of content and emotion. When we understand what God wants, then we will seek to please Him, not ourselves or others.

Balanced worship challenges worshipers:

• Get involved. Participate in worship, whether privately or corporately, with your whole self—emotions and intellect.

• Sing and pray from your heart, not just with your head.

• Listen and learn, not just with the head but also from the heart.

Balanced worship challenges worship leaders:

• Don't yield to the temptation to emphasize worship to the extent that you de-emphasize the proclamation of the Word of God. Allow quality time for the sermon.

• Provide options in worship styles. Whether you incorporate everything into one traditional worship service or offer a separate contemporary service, lead your congregation in balancing their worship. Include music from hymns, Gospel songs, and praise songs. The hymns remind us of our great heritage and teach doctrine of the faith. Gospel songs enable us to hear words of testimony and join in proclaiming them. Praise songs address God directly and make worship real and personal.

If our heads and our hearts are "into" our worship, can our lives be far behind? The balance we are building must be carried out of the context of corporate worship and personal worship into a way-of-life worship. Now the heart that beats day in and day out becomes a striking reminder of how we are then to live. Our heart is not to beat for worship weekends only. Could you survive if your heart stopped and started according to the day of the week, the event scheduled, the place you are at that moment? Of course not. Neither can the heart of worship.

GOING DEEPER
(A Personal Study Guide)

Part 1—Getting into the Word

Prayer—There is no doubt that we are closing in on issues of the heart and not just our "holy habits." With this chapter the need for balance is emphasized, looking at how both heart and head are involved in worship. Pray for the holy balance of contemplation and celebration.

Reading/Hearing God's Word—Read or listen to Psalm 95. Notice the transition that follows verses 1–5: from "shout aloud" to "bow down." Notice also the exhortation that begins at the end of verse 7: "Today, if you hear his voice . . ." If we hear God's voice, we will not harden our hearts.

Understanding God's Word—Read the psalm again. Underline any key phrases or ideas. Then answer the following questions:

1. If you were called on to summarize verses 1–7 in one concise sentence, what would you say? Write it down to keep focused.

_____

_____

_____

2. What are the "reasons" for shouting (vv. 3–4)?

_____

_____

_____

3. What are the "reasons" for bowing (v. 7)?

_____

_____

_____

4. Why do verses 3 and 4 elicit a response of "shouting" while verse 7 encourages the response of "bowing"?

_____

_____

_____

Meditating on God's Word—Psalm 95:6 suggests a kneeling posture. Place your Bible, open to Psalm 95, on a chair in front of you and kneel while you read it again. Then pray, asking God to help you live out this psalm all of the time.

Part 2—The Word in Review

Introduction

> Just as a coach encourages his team, so exhortation to praise involves both emotion and intellect.

I. There Is to Be a Balance of Emotion in Our Worship (Ps. 95:1–7)

> A. Get fired up! (v. 5)
> B. Stay focused! (vv. 6–7)

II. There Is to Be a Balance of Content in Our Worship (John 4:23–24)

> A. Put your heart into it!
> B. Use your head!

Part 3—Taking the Word into My World

There are four key phrases in this lesson, two relating to Psalm 95 and two relating to John 4. All four are important as they remind us of the need for balance in emotion and content. To a certain extent there may appear to be some overlap, so do not try to draw sharp lines of distinction. The goal is to learn that true worship blends all of these elements.

Review the chapter, then write in your own words how you can incorporate that idea into your worship.

From Psalm 95:

Get fired up: _____

Stay focused: _____

From John 4:

Put your heart into it: _____

Use your head: _____

Part 4—Grabbing Hold

Study the following grid. Where would you place yourself? To the left is contemplation and to the right is celebration; at the top is spirit and at the bottom is truth. If you are more contemplation-oriented, the dot will be to the left of the midline. If you are more truth-oriented, then the dot will be below the midline. After evaluating where you stand and marking it with a dot, place an "X" where you think you should be. Now ask yourself, "What is needed to move me from my present position to a well-rounded experience of worship?"

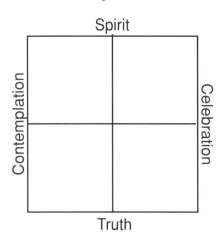

CHAPTER 8

THE PRAISE OF OUR LIVES

Romans 12:1

"True worship can only take place when we agree to God sitting not only on His throne in the center of the universe, but on the throne that stands in the center of our heart."
—Robert Colman

"I think you made a mistake on my bill. . . ." You can feel the tension mounting, see the hair bristling on the back of the waiter's neck. He's ready to take you on, until he hears what you have on your mind. "I don't think you charged me enough for my burger."

Eyebrows arch, eyes widen, the facial expression changes from indignation to disbelief. "Uh . . . I didn't?"

Is this a familiar scene? Or is it just the reverse? You've been overcharged so many times, this little incident just settles the score. What about that scanner at the supermarket that shortchanged you for the day-old bread? Or the time you paid for a dozen bagels and found only eleven in the bag when you got home? Now, for once, the mistake is in your favor, so you just pocket the change, thinking, *It's about time.*

But if you are truly seeking to live all of life in response to God, you will choose the spiritual reaction rather than the worldly rationalization. It is in those kinds of settings and situations that worship is made real and our hearts are revealed.

Worship is more than attending services—or even participating in them. It is more than spending time with God, one-on-one. When understood in its broadest, fullest sense, worship is living the entirety of our life in response to Him. Who God is, what He says, and what He does so affect us that every moment of our day is viewed through a mental grid of worship.

The Anglo-Saxon word *weorthscipe* (*worth-ship*), from which *worship* is derived, tells us about the concept of worthiness. God alone is worthy of our praise and sacrifice. But our view of Him may be warped and skewed. As we ascribe to God His true worth, then our attitudes, actions, and offerings are all affected. We declare God's worth by allowing Him to influence every part of our life. Ascribing worth is worship. Showing God that we value Him so much that all of life is brought into conformity with His will is worship.

Consider how what you value affects the way you live. If your most prized possession is your flower garden, then the books you read, the places you visit, how you spend your money, the use of your time, and your circle of friends and acquaintances will reflect your passion. You will read about flower gardens—how to pick the right plants for your location, instructions on arranging their placement for maximum beauty, and tips on the care and feeding of annuals and perennials. An afternoon drive might be more of a scouting expedition to study landscaping done by professionals or to visit your favorite nurseries. Parks offer lavish displays of plant life, and some gardens are tourist attractions in themselves.

The point can also be made for an interest in cars, or quilts, or football, or coin collecting . . . and the list goes on. Whatever you value, you assign worth, and the greater the perceived worth, the more it affects your life.

The same is true of our assessment of God. The more worth or value we assign to Him, the more He will occupy our attention, affect how we live, and be able to transform our lives.

Whole-Life Worship

In the Book of Romans, Paul writes of God's amazing grace in Christ. Because of His sacrifice, you and I can know, with absolute certainty, that our sins are forgiven! No wonder Paul breaks into a doxology at the conclusion of chapter 11:

"Oh, the depth of the riches of the wisdom and knowledge of God! How unsearchable his judgments, and his paths beyond tracing out! 'Who has known the mind of the Lord? Or who has been his counselor?' 'Who has ever given to God, that God should repay him?' For from him and through him and to him are all things. To him be the glory forever! Amen" (vv. 33–36).

Our worship of God should never be separated from our belief about God. "On the one hand, there can be no doxology without theology," writes John Stott. "It is not possible to worship an unknown god. . . . On the other hand, there should be no theology without doxology. There is something fundamentally flawed about a purely academic interest in God."[1]

You can't skip to the back of the book and understand Romans. You must read the first eleven chapters—how to know God (theology)—to form a basis for worshiping Him (doxology). Taken alone, the concluding verses of Romans 11 are a magnificent statement of worship. Taken as part of the Book of Romans, they form a bridge connecting theology with real life.

Notice the small but significant first word of Romans 12: *therefore*. What Paul says from that point on flows out of the preceding eleven chapters. God, through the apostle, is calling us to a life of service that issues from our understanding of Him and our praise of Him. If we know God, we will want to praise Him; knowing God results in worship. As we praise Him, we will be led to serve Him; our lives will become conduits of service.

The real conclusion to the first eleven chapters of Romans is not 11:33–36 but 12:1 and following, a truth obscured by what is possibly the worst chapter break in the Bible, one that allows us too easily to separate theology from life. It may have been Bishop Moule who warned that we must "beware equally of an undevotional theology and of an untheological devotion."[2]

It is so easy to stop with the doxology. We're saved! Praise God! So easy, yet so incomplete, so self-centered. There is more for us to know, more for us to do. It is precisely at this point that Paul says, "Therefore, I urge you, brothers, in view of

God's mercy, to offer your bodies as living sacrifices, holy and pleasing to God—this is your spiritual act of worship."

Paul's call for commitment is based upon God's mercy. We owe to God everything we have and are because of it. Mercy is that quality in God that moves Him to deliver us from sin, evil, and self. Mercy is used here as the leverage for the appeal that follows. While some religious systems teach that sacrifices are made in order to *gain* mercy, biblical Christianity teaches that sacrifice is to be *our response to* mercy. Worship is not what we do to gain mercy, but what we do because we have already received it. The more we understand what God has done for us, the greater our commitment should be.

In these opening verses of chapter 12, we find a call to sacrifice, a call to service, and a call to a lifestyle of worship.

A Call to Sacrificial Living

The sacrifice we are called to make is not some liturgy or ritual—some empty form—but the offering of our bodies. To present our bodies is a thoroughly inclusive concept. They represent all that we are—our career, our relationships with family and friends, our work in the community where we live, our responsibilities in the state and nation in which we are citizens, and the world we touch in travel and missions work. We are to sacrifice—to let go of—everything that is *us*!

The next three phrases help us define the kind of sacrifice the Lord requires:

A living sacrifice. Sacrifices are usually viewed in terms of death. In Old Testament times, the lamb (or bull or goat) was brought to the altar and slaughtered. The contrast between that image of sacrifice and the one we are called to is more than night and day—it is death and life. This kind of sacrifice dies to self and lives to become more like Christ day by day.

As some like to point out, however, it is easier to be a dead sacrifice than a living one. The dead sacrifice has to make the decision to die only once, whereas living sacrifices must continually lay down plans and ambitions, dreams and destiny. The problem with living sacrifices is that they have the tendency to keep crawling off the altar!

I have never cooked lobster, but one of my daughters wishes I would learn. You know, buy one of those live creatures they keep in the tanks at the grocery, claws banded shut, then drop it headfirst into a pot of boiling water! Not my idea of an enjoyable evening in the kitchen. Besides, I am not overly enthusiastic about reaching into a grocery bag and pulling out anything live! What if it gets loose? In its lobster-sized mind, it might not understand the physics of boiling, but it does understand the need to escape from the source of the heat!

The analogy breaks down, of course, when considering the theology of worship. God does not drop us into a place of certain death just to evoke praise from our lips. But we do tend to try to squirm out of the difficult places, to crawl off the altar, so to speak, especially when He turns up the heat.

Nevertheless, we are to spend every day of our lives with every breath praising and glorifying God as living sacrifices.

A holy sacrifice. In its most basic sense, the word *holy* speaks of that which is separated from the profane and dedicated to the service of the Lord. To be holy moves one out of the ways of the world in which we live and into the ways of the God we serve. Our lives then become set apart for His purposes.

Holiness implies both a negative and a positive. We are no longer in the grip of sin, but in the grip of grace. We make ourselves available to God, who has saved and delivered us from our former lifestyle of self. In gratitude, we now desire to please Him, to be acceptable to Him.

Imagine sitting down at the table for a meal. A place has been set for you. It is "set apart" for you—holy, in a sense. Suppose you looked at the plate and saw the remnants of previous meals. If you were in a restaurant, you would call the waiter and complain. Now imagine the waiter saying, "Is there a problem? We set this place for you. It is set aside and available for you. What more could you want?"

The answer would be obvious. "I want a clean plate."

Being set aside and being available are only two-thirds of what makes a person holy. We must also be acceptable to God.

A pleasing sacrifice. Sacrifice is not judged on the basis of what we think, but what God thinks. The acceptability of a sacrifice is His decision, not ours. It is God who pronounces it pleasing, or good, not us.

When you become a living sacrifice that is holy and pleasing to God, you may be tempted to think in terms of what you are giving up. That may not be altogether bad. Perhaps some questionable thoughts and activities need to be jettisoned from your life in order for you to be pure before the Lord. Other things, good in themselves, may not be God's best for you, or you may be put on hold according to His timetable. You will give up those good things to gain something better. The "better" life—staying in and doing the will of God—is lived on the altar. And as a living sacrifice, every place you go becomes your altar.

In our day we do not typically experience literal sacrifice. Such an act is a shocking concept. A bleating sheep, a sharp knife, a slicing of the jugular, a rush of warm blood, a last feeble movement, a sudden release of life. We would prefer to think of sacrifice in baseball terms—say, a fly ball hit to the outfield to advance a runner.

Consider, however, the ultimate Sacrifice—Jesus Christ, the Son of the living God. Read again His prayer in the garden of Gethsemane. Can there be any doubt that He knew the reality of the word *sacrifice*, that He would lay down His life—not just figuratively, but on a roughly hewn wooden cross? We will never be called to anything comparable to Calvary, but we are called to sacrificial living.

This Is Our Spiritual Act of Worship

The last phrase of Romans 12:1—"this is your spiritual act of worship"—confronts us with the issue of whole-life worship. Living sacrifices give their whole lives; it is not an on-again, off-again arrangement. Living sacrifices live lives of service, not once in awhile, but always, all the time.

The word translated "spiritual" is the Greek word *logiken*, from which we get our word *logic*. Some scholars prefer to translate it here as "reasonable." In light of all that God has done for us, it is only reasonable that we would respond with a life of service. Either translation is acceptable. Our sacrifice is to be intelligent and deliberate—reasonable—but it is much more than the logical outcome of a relationship. It is a sacrifice made to serve God, offered in view of the sacrifice He made for our salvation, that moves our decision into the realm of the spiritual.

Our service is a spiritual service, a sacrifice of all that we are, offered to God as a holy sacrifice. This is a spiritual act of worship, made rationally and logically, not just emotionally.

The other key word in this phrase is *latpreia*, translated "worship." This word can also be translated "service, ministry, offering, or sacrifice." But "worship" says it all.

Try reading the verse backwards: "Here is your act of worship, which is spiritual." Your worship is the sacrifice of your "body"—all that you are. God is not asking you to commit suicide, but to live fully and abundantly in all that He has for you.

While driving down the road one day, I glanced in the rearview mirror only to see the reflection of a police car. What would have been your reaction? Probably the same as mine. Instinctively, I glanced at the speedometer to check my speed, took my foot off the accelerator, and braked slightly. Call it reflex action. Call it a guilty conscience. But for whatever reason, I responded to the presence behind me.

My response to a superior authority was, in essence, an act of worship. That officer had the delegated authority to clock my speed, pull me over, and give me a ticket, if necessary. That fact stimulated the appropriate response. In fact, it caused me to evaluate other areas of vehicular law besides observing the speed limit: signaling before making a turn, keeping the proper distance between my car and the vehicle in front of me, and double-checking to be sure that my seat belt was buckled!

Now change the scenario a bit. Imagine glancing in the rearview mirror and seeing God. What would you do next? Wouldn't knowing that He was right there behind you affect your thoughts, your actions, your decisions?

Well, He is there. Always. Whether you're driving your car, working at your desk, mowing the lawn, talking to a waitress, surfing the Web, or playing catch with your kids. The more you live in the awareness of God, the more you will desire to live a holy, acceptable life—which is only reasonable, after all.

Making It Real

The rearview mirror illustration helps us understand what it means to live in response to God. Take the following test and see how well you measure up:

• You are going through the checkout line at the grocery store and are undercharged for an item. Are you as quick to point out the oversight to the cashier as you are when you are overcharged?

• A waitress leaves an item off the bill. Do you let it go, pleased that the meal cost less because of her mistake, or do you call her back to the table and explain the error, knowing it will cost you more?

• You are filling out your income tax and know that changing a figure or two can mean a greater refund. Can you honestly sign that statement at the bottom of the page, the one that asks if all the information is accurate, honest, truthful?

Being worshipers of God affects the way we pay our bills, treat our neighbors, deal with businesspeople, and compute our taxes.

People who practice whole-life worship are a delight to be around. For one thing, you don't have to worry about being cheated or betrayed. They aren't going to gossip or backbite. They will build you up, not tear you down. They will love and encourage. They will serve as salt and light.

Look in the rearview mirror. Someone is watching and listening. As a child of God, your worship is showing.

GOING DEEPER
(A Personal Study Guide)

Part 1—Getting into the Word

Prayer—Sometimes familiarity breeds something other than contempt—it breeds "overlooking." We too easily fly past familiar texts. Ask God to help you meditate on Romans 12:1, looking for fresh insights and application for your life today.

Reading/Hearing God's Word—Read or listen to Romans 11:33–36. The doxology of 12:1 flows from the theology of the first eleven chapters of this book.

Understanding God's Word—Read Romans 11:33–12:1. Watch for verses or ideas that are especially meaningful to you today. In particular, look for things that relate to why being a living sacrifice is logical/reasonable in light of what God has done for us. Then answer the following questions:

1. An Old Testament sacrifice was made at the tabernacle, or later at the temple. Where is the altar on which living sacrifices are offered today?

_____

_____

_____

2. Some of the Old Testament sacrifices were made at specific times or in conjunction with specific events. What are the times and events for living sacrifices today?

_____

_____

_____

Meditating on God's Word—Read Romans 12:1 in reverse: "Here is your act of worship, which is spiritual." Your worship is your sacrifice of your body—not by killing it but by living your life as God would have you live it. Notice the word *your*

113

and consider the implications of each of those phrases—"your worship, your sacrifice, your body, your life." Then consider what God is asking you to do.

Part 2—The Word in Review

Introduction

> The suggested scenario at the beginning of this chapter reminds us that true worship may be observed wherever we are and whatever we're doing.

I. Whole-Life Worship (Rom. 12:1)

II. A Call to Sacrificial Living (12:1)

    A. A living sacrifice
    B. A holy sacrifice
    C. A pleasing sacrifice

III. Our Spiritual Act of Worship (12:1)

Part 3—Taking the Word into My World

Worship begins on the inside, then spills over on the outside— not the other way around. For a living sacrifice, every place is an altar and every moment a potential opportunity for offering service to God.

In each of the major phrases in Romans 12:1 below, ask, "What does this mean for me?" It may mean that there are questionable activities or thoughts that need to be removed from your life and others added. Some areas require strengthening, while others, de-emphasizing.

1. A living sacrifice

_____

2. A holy sacrifice

_____

3. A pleasing sacrifice

_____

4. My spiritual act of worship

_____

In what way(s) will your life be different when you carry your worship into every area of your world?

Part 4—Grabbing Hold

Write out an action plan—specific steps you are going to take to make worship real in your life. Your list may include such "resolutions" as, "I will be honest in my business dealings. I will always tell the truth and resist the temptation to use the euphemistic 'little white lie.'"

Cover such areas as corporate worship, personal worship/ devotions, involvement in discipleship and disciple-making. Add to your list as your life reflects more perfectly your response to God dwelling in you.

CHAPTER 9

THE MOST IMPORTANT THING

Nehemiah 12:27–43

"We are often so caught up in our activities that we tend to worship our work, work at our play, and play at our worship."
—Charles Swindoll

The question seemed innocent enough. Thought-provoking, yes, but not offensive. It was the speediness of the answer that was surprising. The woman had asked, "What is the most important thing in worship?"

In a time in which worship has become so narrowly defined, it would seem that the most important thing in worship might be just that—some *thing*. Something to say. Something to do. Something to become. The most important thing in worship is _____ (you fill in the blank).

Singing, which is often equated with worship, might be one response. The worship band plays during the worship time, which begins with the worship leader saying, "Let's worship now as we sing." Other answers might include the person's heart attitude, bowing down, and bringing a sacrifice of praise. All of these are involved in our worship.

But Colin Owen did not have to ponder his reply to the woman's question about the most important aspect of worship. His answer came instantly and carried profound weight. It was simply this: "To do it." He continues, "We as a church have lost sight of what real worship is. Don't believe me? Then look in your Bible for a verse that says worship is musical. If you find one, please let me know."[1]

The truth may well be that at the top of the list—music, prayer, sermon, offerings—should be the words, "Do it!" We may know the elements and know them well, but leave out the most important part—to put them into practice.

Hopefully, by now our understanding of worship has expanded to include both the narrow view—giving adoration to God—and the broad view—understanding worship as a way of life—and that both begin in the heart. Hopefully, the words of Jesus have instructed us to worship in spirit and in truth, the example of Nehemiah has challenged us to work on our worship life, and the psalmist has convinced us that a life of worship needs the proper balance of intellect and emotion. Hopefully, we are determined daily to die to ourselves and become living sacrifices, which is our spiritual act of worship. And hopefully we don't just talk about it—we do it!

As living sacrifices, we recognize that worship is not about us, but about God. It is what we give to Him, not what we get for ourselves. As John MacArthur points out, "Modern Christianity seems committed . . . to the idea that God should be giving to us. God does give to us abundantly, but we need to understand the balance of that truth—we are to render honor and adoration to God. That consuming, self-less desire to give to God is the essence and the heart of wor-ship. It begins with the giving first of ourselves, and then of our attitudes, and then of our possessions—until worship is a way of life."[2]

When researching worship scenes in the Bible, we turn almost instinctively to the books of John and Isaiah and Revelation, but seldom to the Book of Nehemiah. Yet, as we have already discovered, this book is concerned with far more than building a wall. Nehemiah was not applauding the skills and abilities of the stonemasons of Jerusalem, but the charac-ter of God. In fact, a great percentage of his record details the worship service held to dedicate the rebuilt wall. God was glorified that day.

The People Paused . . . (v. 27)

The narrative of Nehemiah moves at a measured pace. In chapter 1 he hears of the sad state of affairs in his native Jerusalem—charred gates, broken walls, a city in disgrace—and it drives him to his knees. In the next chapter, Nehemiah recites his prayer once more before King Artaxerxes and enlists the king's aid in returning to his homeland. God's gracious hand is upon Nehemiah as he sets out to accomplish his divine assignment. When opposition to the rebuilding arises, Nehemiah answers his critics with assurance and faith in God. When the laborers grow tired and defeated, he encourages them with reminders of God's provision of mercy and assistance.

All this in less than half the book! If Nehemiah was about building programs, the book would have ended here. But over and over again, it is all about God. The remaining chapters show the centrality of God in the lives of His people and their response to Him in worship. The Word was read, sins confessed, and when the rebuilding was completed, a dedication service was held. The people took time away from their duties and stepped back from their daily tasks to celebrate.

They paused . . . to worship.

Worship takes time. Our lives can feel as if the fast-forward button is stuck in the "on" position. Computers, PDAs, wireless technology—all contribute to the ever-quickening tempo of life. We put wheels on our suitcases—not only to make them easier to carry, but to help us travel faster. We purchase the largest carry-on allowed, put wheels on it, cram it full, bypass the baggage claim area, hit the ground with cell phone to ear, and hightail it to our next destination.

We need to hit the pause button. Yet the idea of pausing for anything is almost unheard of today. Drivers coast through stop signs, fly through yellow lights, and head to drive-through windows for everything from Big Macs to minor surgery. Our lives are filled with things to do, places to go, people to see. Life is lived at a frenetic pace. What can get lost in the shuffle is our worship and quiet times alone with God.

Do you pause regularly, often, individually, corporately to bask in the presence of the One who knows you best and loves you most?

The People Prepared Themselves for Worship (vv. 27–30)

The details of the dedication service are evidence that this was no haphazard get-together, but a carefully planned event. Preparation involved more than putting together an order of service and calling the participants together. It included preparation of the worshipers themselves, an often sadly neglected aspect of worship today.

The preparation required planning. Two groups of people—the Levites and the musicians—were recruited from the various regions where they lived and brought to Jerusalem. Both would play a significant part in the special occasion.

They had a clear purpose—"to celebrate joyfully" (v. 27). There was good reason to celebrate; God had been at work in their lives! But their accomplishment was not the only source of their joy. God Himself caused joy to well up in them that day. But before they could express it, there was much work to be done.

Imagine the multitude of details that had to be orchestrated prior to the event: parades to be planned, choirs rehearsed, songs of thanksgiving assigned, instrumental music selected. The instructions were very specific; for example, the choir was to be divided into two parts. These singers would process on the top of the wall—one group to the right, the other to the left—until they met. Thus, the entire city would be surrounded with the sound of music! Obviously, such a display would require elaborate preparation. This was not a spontaneous "while we're together, let's just praise the Lord."

And then there were the offerings. Sacrificial animals had to be selected and corralled. Arrangements made for the ceremony. Tools and instruments prepared.

There is a tension that can exist between planning and spontaneity. Yes, we allow for the leading of God in worship, but we also recognize that He is a God of order, of excellence. He is meticulous in His instructions. Too often, spontaneity can be an excuse for laziness. What we do in His service should reflect His character and glory. Either extreme—over-planning or under-planning—carries with it potential hazards to our relationship with the Lord.

Some suggest we need to allow flexibility in our worship so that the Holy Spirit is free to work in our midst. At the other end of the spectrum are those who, with stopwatch in hand, carefully script, even choreograph every move of a service. Nothing is to deviate from the predetermined plan. No prayer goes too long, no song verses repeated unless agreed upon in advance, lights dimmed at the precise moment, the order of service strictly observed.

Which is best? May I be so bold as to say, "Neither." The best is usually not found at the extremes but in the "betweens." The Spirit works on Tuesday as well as on Sunday. Special music can be coordinated in advance with the message. The flow and sequence of the service can be developed and a unified, thematic service can be anticipated—while allowing for the Spirit to break through the brick walls of our prearranged program.

Once, while in another country, another culture, I was reminded of this as I sat in a service waiting to speak. Although there was some order to the service, it had not been communicated to me, so I sat at the front, watching intently, trying to anticipate when I was to speak. The soloist finished, seemingly a certain indication that I was next. As I listened to her song, I found myself writing down the words of the chorus because they fit so well with my message. This was not due to any planning on our part since I had arrived in the country only twelve hours earlier.

There was a moment of confusion on the platform. Someone was being told, "Not now." Then I was introduced.

I began my sermon, and in spite of having jotted down the chorus on my notes, I failed to mention it at the conclusion of my message. After a closing prayer, I sat down and looked on curiously as another soloist came to the platform. The "plan" had been for back-to-back solos, but the worship leader had "spontaneously" changed it. The second song fit like glove and hand with both the first song and the message!

Could we have planned it better? Probably not. Could we

have messed it up by being inflexible? Definitely! I sat in thankful wonder as the worship leader explained that quick decision to postpone the one song until after the message. "Now I know," he said, "why the Spirit was prompting me to do that." It was a combination of planning and spontaneity, one that pleased God and was a blessing to the people.

The preparation involved purification. Another aspect of the preparation for the ceremony was purification—a ritual cleansing from impure objects or activities in order to enter the presence of the holy God; to do otherwise meant death. This purification was not running the vacuum down the carpet of the center aisle, or a Saturday night bath, or putting on their "Sunday-go-to-meetin" clothes, but a spiritual purification.

Old Testament purification rites took various forms, involving water, blood, and fire. Note that those who would be leading the dedication service—the priests and Levites—were required to purify themselves first (v. 30). They had to bathe and put on clean garments. Only then would they be qualified to purify the people, the gates, and the walls.

These physical actions of purification, reminders of both the need for purity and God's willingness to purify, helped prepare their hearts for serving Him. Holiness was not something for others, but for all people—*beginning in the house of the Lord*. It was not an option, but a requirement. Not a ritual only, but a necessary act.

Those who lead God's people in worship must be holy themselves. Those who participate in worship are also expected to come before God with "clean hands and a pure heart" (Ps. 24:4). Purification is not just a cleaning up on the outside but a cleansing on the inside as well.

A typical weakness is coming to worship unprepared. The service may have been planned, even printed in the worship folder, but the people gather with no more forethought than to set the alarm on Saturday night. Of course, preparation for Sunday worship should include physical preparation. Part of that is getting the rest needed to be mentally alert.

Our personal preparation should also include the spiritual. The better we emotionally prepare for something, the better the time will be. While preparing the heart spiritually is not altogether an emotional experience, it is a necessary part. Remember, we are to worship "in spirit and in truth." Time spent reading the Bible and praying can be vital to preparing our hearts.

Making Sunday morning a quieter, calmer time can help. Planning what to wear, keeping the television off, listening to worship music while dressing, leaving with time to spare to eliminate the rush, setting things out the night before rather than searching frantically that morning—all are things that can be part of our preparation to worship. While they may seem a curious blend of physical routines and spiritual, both work together to compose the mind and heart.

What we do to prepare for worship shows the priority of God in our lives. Consider the time and effort spent in preparing Thanksgiving dinner for your family or throwing a birthday party for a special friend. Look what some fans do before a big sports event—don the team colors, decorate their faces, make special foods, create a pep rally atmosphere—all to prepare for what is ultimately only a game.

The people of Nehemiah's day knew the importance of coming to "the holy hill" fully prepared to worship. Unholy worshipers before the holy God? It was unacceptable then and it is unacceptable now.

The People Participated in Worship (vv. 31–43)

Worship was not a spectator sport for the people at the dedication of the wall. The combination of the choirs, instruments, and rejoicing produced a sound of joy that could be heard even at a great distance (v. 43). "The singers sang loud," says the *King James Version* (v. 42). "The singers made themselves heard" is the literal translation of that verse. There is no question that music—loud and extravagant music, in this case—was a vital element in the worship that day.

Ten of the verses in Nehemiah 12:27–43 mention music. As the people participated, they did so by singing with great joy — and with great volume. God had worked to bring laborers and materials together to rebuild the wall. He had protected and prospered them. They had plenty to shout about!

J. I. Packer calls the time of the dedication service "a day of uninhibited delight." He also cautions that, "Exuberance, carnival-style, can easily become carnal and unspiritual, but surely the exalted intensity of this day of worship, an exalted intensity that finds expression in many of the Psalms, has something to say to us today."[3]

When our team wins, the cheers come easily. Yet the same person who yells from the top of the stadium on a Saturday afternoon may mumble a song, almost inaudibly, on Sunday. That is in contrast to the people in Jerusalem that day. They were not content to sit idly by. Their participation was the whole-body variety.

In the Old Testament, people sang, shouted, stood, knelt, bowed, clapped their hands, raised their hands, and danced. Nowhere in God's Word do we read that they simply sat as they worshiped. God is the One who sits enthroned. The worshipers kneel or stand before Him in a gesture of praise, adoration, submission, and servitude.

We know that worship is not just a matter of body position or words and music; it is also our attitudes, actions, and offerings. Old Testament worship included sacrifices, "great sacrifices," according to verse 43. To receive these offerings, men were appointed to be in charge of the storerooms for the contributions of the people. Here they brought their firstfruits and tithes into the temple, as required by the Word of God.

Our worship of God must also include the gifts that we bring and the sacrifices we make. Not animal sacrifices, as in Old Testament times, but time, talents, and possessions. We are also taught to give to the support of God's work, regularly, proportionally, as He has prospered us. Worship that does not include giving is incomplete.

So, then, worship is not something we observe; it is something we do. The people on the platform are not performers we watch; they are prompters, there to encourage us to participate in worship.

What God had done in Nehemiah's life, in the heart of a king, and among a group of people resulted in the wall of Jerusalem being rebuilt. The people responded in worship. They paused, prepared, and participated in a great event, one in which they exalted the Lord with everything they had.

Worship requires pushing the pause button; God deserves our praise, our time, our resources, our energy. We should plan, not only corporately but individually, to make our times of worship meaningful and significant. To get involved, not as passive spectators, but as full participants with the words that we sing, the prayers that we pray, and the offerings that we bring. With all of our hearts. With all of our lives.

Making It Real

This scene from Nehemiah gives us a very specific model to follow. This does not mean that we must always split the choir, walk around the roof of the church, and meet in the middle. But it does suggest some very specific ways in which we can become involved in worship:

• **Evaluate your worship time.** Do you push the "pause button" daily for personal times of worship, weekly for corporate times of worship—or is this done only "weakly"? It will not just happen. Just as you will not one day wake up with a disciplined workout schedule, you will not gain a discipline of worship accidentally. It is gained intentionally. To pause, you must plan.

• **Prepare yourself personally.** Come before God with "clean hands and a pure heart." That may require confession and repentance. You wipe your feet before entering the house and wash your hands before eating, don't you? You get cleaned up before a special event and clean up before "company" comes. Of far greater significance is the cleaning up of your heart and life as you prepare to worship.

• **Get involved.** "Don't just sit there, do something!" Sing to the best of your ability. Listen intently. Pray along with those who lead in prayer. Be open and receptive to the teaching of the Word of God.

In worshiping God, whether personally or corporately, you are giving Him only what He deserves. Give Him your songs, give Him your tithes and offerings, give Him your time, give Him your talents. But the most important thing is . . . do it. He alone is worthy!

GOING DEEPER
(A Personal Study Guide)

Part 1—Getting into the Word

Prayer—As you begin this study, ask God to speak to you through His Word. Then be prepared to do what He asks. It is one thing to know what to do; it is still another to do what God wants. Pray that He will give you a greater desire to be obedient.

Reading/Hearing God's Word—Read or listen to Nehemiah 12:27–47, being alert to verses or ideas that are especially relevant to your life. Keep in mind that the people of Nehemiah's day had been involved in a great work of God. What had probably seemed highly unlikely, if not impossible, was accomplished in a remarkably short period of time. Now it was time to worship. As you read, consider the fact that they left all the items on their to-do list yet remaining and took time for the most important thing—worship.

Understanding God's Word—Reread the passage from Nehemiah. This exercise is not redundant, but intended to increase your grasp of the text. Now answer the following questions:

1. We have already learned that worship involves attitude, actions, and offerings. In what ways is each of these demonstrated in this worship time?

_____

_____

_____

2. Describe the musical portion of this praise service. Note the variety of instruments and choirs as well as the people involved and how they participated.

_____

_____

_____

Meditating on God's Word—Write a brief summary of a meaningful verse or idea from this passage. Perhaps there is a desire in your heart to worship God in a joyous way, recognizing His great work in your life.

_____

_____

_____

Part 2—The Word in Review

Introduction

The most important thing in worship is to do it

I. The People Paused for Worship (Neh. 12:27)

II. The People Prepared Themselves for Worship (vv. 27–30)

A. The preparation involved planning
B. The preparation involved purification

III. The People Participated in Worship (vv. 31–43)

A. The worship included music
B. The worship included sacrifices
C. The worship included the sound of rejoicing

Part 3—Taking the Word into My World

Perhaps this is the most significant juncture we can encounter in the process of developing the heart God desires. You probably began reading this book because you already were interested in or somewhat knowledgeable about worship. Now you realize that it is not enough to know—you must also "do" worship.

Evaluate your life on each of the points of this chapter:

1. Do you pause for worship? Consider how your time is used. Review your schedule to see if there is any regularity to personal and corporate times of worship. How consistent are you in living worship as a way of life?

_____

_____

_____

2. Do you prepare for worship? While more than 90 percent of all churchgoing adults view worship as their number-one priority, less than half prepare themselves for worship. What are specific steps you can take to prepare for corporate worship? In the same way, what do you do to prepare for personal worship?

_____

_____

_____

3. Do you participate in worship, both individually and corporately? Do you literally sing God's praises? Do you exalt His name? Do you testify to others of His goodness and mercy? Consider what sacrifices (time, possessions, talents) you offer to God.

_____

_____

_____

Part 4—Grabbing Hold

Now get specific:

1. This week I will pause for worship at the following time(s):

_____

_____

2. This week I will prepare for corporate worship by:

_____

_____

3. This week I will prepare for personal worship by:

_____

_____

Put these three action steps to work in your life, and you will find yourself growing the heart of worship God desires.

CHAPTER 10

UNACCEPTABLE WORSHIP

Selected Scriptures

"The holy art of worship seems to have passed away like the Shekinah glory from the tabernacle. As a result, we are left to our own devices and forced to make up the lack of spontaneous worship by bringing in countless cheap and tawdry activities to hold the attention of the church people."
—A. W. Tozer

In our family, pizza is not just something we eat occasionally. It is an inalienable right ranking up there with "life, liberty, and the pursuit of happiness." If it is Friday, then we eat pizza. One week I even told the cashier at the pizza place, "We'll be out of town next Friday. I thought I'd mention it so you wouldn't wonder if something had happened to us."

We are rather basic in our approach to pizza, typically getting two of them, one topping each. My favorite happens to be Italian sausage.

So, just suppose it's Friday night and I have stopped by to pick up my order. The person at the counter recognizes me, goes immediately to the pick-up area, grabs the box with my name on it, and says, "Here's your anchovy pizza!"

"But I didn't order anchovy—I ordered Italian sausage," I complain.

"Yes, but anchovy is the kind *I* like best," he replies.

Do you think I would put up with that? Of course not. I knew exactly what I wanted when I placed my order, and I wouldn't settle for a substitute, particularly someone else's favorite.

A similar situation happens all too often in worship. Most of us tend to worship God in the style to which we have become accustomed or which best suits our personality or preference. We may even expect God to be grateful that we're worshiping at all! Wrong.

Some of our ideas about God, how we perceive Him, and our approaches to worship — based on our wishes, not His will — are simply unacceptable. Just as we would not accept any other kind of pizza when we'd specifically ordered what we wanted, so God does not accept any and all worship. If we are truly to make worship a way of life, then it must be a life of worship that is acceptable to Him, not one that is first and foremost pleasing to ourselves.

In an anything-goes world, some people have a casual attitude toward worship as well. Understanding what is and is not acceptable to God will bring us to a decision point. Either we will seek to please Him or to please ourselves. And if we choose the latter, we are no longer worshiping God but serving self, putting what we desire above what God requires.

Throughout this book, we have examined various worship scenes. Some of them — Isaiah's vision in the year that King Uzziah died, for example — are striking and dramatic. Fantastic! Awesome! Give us more!

Other worship scenes found in the Bible are less conspicuous, hardly noticeable as the story unfolds. One of these is Gideon's foray into the Midianite camp, where he overheard some of the soldiers talking about a dream in which Gideon won the victory. There, in that moment, standing outside the enemy tent, Gideon worshiped. As did Peter when he got back in the boat after walking on the water to reach Jesus.

On the other hand, we may altogether overlook those accounts where worship was inappropriate and unacceptable to God. We tend to concentrate on the other lessons we can learn from these worship scenes while missing the important truth that *God is very specific* about what He desires in worship.

The One We Worship (Ex. 20:3)

Number one on God's list of Ten Commandments is, "'You shall have no other gods before me'" (Ex. 20:3). All the commandments are important, yet there is a special signifi-cance to the prohibition against having any other god but the true God.

The stone tablets upon which God wrote the Ten Commandments with His own finger did not last long. As Moses was descending from Mount Sinai and saw the golden calf the people had carved in their impatience to get on with their worship, his anger "burned" and he threw the tablets, breaking them into pieces (32:19).

God replaced the broken tablets. He did not come up with a new set of commandments, but He did inscribe the same commandments on a new set of tablets. Before doing so, He reviewed them with Moses first to make sure He was being understood. It was almost as if He wanted to give added emphasis to His law by going over the high points before writing them down again.

"Do not worship any other god," He said, adding, "for the LORD, whose name is Jealous, is a jealous God" (34:14). It's interesting that in each of the five times the word *jealous* occurs in the Old Testament it refers only to God—a strong indication of the value God places on His relationship with His people.

God knew also that because His people would be sur-rounded by pagan nations, they would be tempted to wor-ship other gods; therefore, the altars, sacred stones, and Asherah poles, along with the wooden poles placed alongside Baal's altar, were to be destroyed.

As the passage continues, God warns against the unholy alliances that would become "snares," actions that lead to idolatry. The people were forbidden from making idols. Notice how He begins this lesson—by reminding them of His character: "[I Am] the compassionate and gracious God, slow to anger, abounding in love and faithfulness, maintaining love to thousands, and forgiving wickedness, rebellion and sin." But read on. "Yet he does not leave the guilty unpun-ished" (vv. 6–7).

The worship of false gods is a serious issue. One of these false gods—wealth—is rather subtle, not as obvious as a statue or icon. "'If I have put my trust in gold or said to pure gold, "You are my security," if I have rejoiced over my great wealth, the fortune my hands had gained, if I have regarded the sun in its radiance or the moon moving in splendor, so that my heart was secretly enticed and my hand offered them a kiss of homage, then these also would be sins to be judged, for I would have been unfaithful to God on high'" (Job 31:24–28).

Greed and idolatry are almost synonymous in these verses; greed can cast gold into a god. Images carved in stone or made of wood, representing pagan deities, are obvious false gods—so obvious that most people are not easily deceived. Materialism, on the other hand, may be slightly more difficult to discern, but it is an idol all the same. When our hearts are captured by things, things become what we value, seek, desire, even worship. When we give more "worth-ship" to the acquisition of material possessions than to God, we are guilty of idolatry!

Our Perception of the One We Worship (Ex. 32:1–8)

It might seem that the account of the golden calf in Exodus 32 is an example of the worship of a false god. While it is an example of the making of an image of God, which is expressly forbidden, in reality it is not an example of worshiping a false god. That day, while wondering what was taking Moses so long on the mountain, Aaron led the people in the worship of the true God in a false form.

"When the people saw that Moses was so long in coming down from the mountain, they gathered around Aaron and said, 'Come, make us *gods* who will go before us. As for this fellow Moses who brought us up out of Egypt, we don't know what has happened to him'" (v. 1).

The Hebrew word translated "gods"—*Elohim*—may also be rendered "God." Sometimes a plural noun is used in the Hebrew to emphasize greatness. This is a grammatical device known as a "plural of majesty." In fact, "God" is most often the translation of this word in the English version of the Old Testament. Either translation of *Elohim* is acceptable, but opinion is divided as to which is intended in this passage. If "gods" is the chosen reading, then the people are guilty of syncretism—in this case, the combination of an idol, an altar, and a celebration of the true God. If "God" is chosen, the passage is an even more forceful example, the verses fitting together smoothly. As the people wonder what happened to God and Moses, they are given an image of God, similar to images of gods in Egypt, and hold a festival of praise to the Lord. They were not worshiping idols, but the true God in an inappropriate form.

Notice carefully the wording in verse 5: "When Aaron saw this [the golden image the people had made], he built an altar in front of the calf and announced, 'Tomorrow there will be a festival to the LORD.'" The Hebrew word *adonai* is translated "lord"; when it refers to God Himself, the word is capitalized—"LORD." But *Adonai* is not the word used in verse 5. Instead, this is yet a third word that refers to God—*Yahweh,* the covenant name of God, the redemptive name that speaks of His unique relationship with His people.

In our worship, we must be committed to the truth. That commitment must be carried into every aspect of our worship—especially in our representation of God. To worship God as we perceive Him instead of how He reveals Himself would be a distortion of the truth. He does not allow us this option.

The Pride That Can Destroy Worship

Proper worship focuses on God Himself. It is what we do to honor and praise Him, to show Him how much we value Him. Somehow, though, we keep getting in the way. Pride demands a piece of the action. Perhaps not blatantly, as in expecting to be worshiped, but a more subtle version, as in "I want to worship my way." While we may not bow down to an idol, we may esteem something we desire or something we enjoy more highly than God. Or, like the unfortunate Israelites whose stories follow, we might decide how we want to worship and insist on doing it our way.

135

Nadab and Abihu (Lev. 10:1–3). "Aaron's sons Nadab and Abihu took their censers, put fire in them and added incense; and they offered unauthorized fire before the LORD, contrary to his command. So fire came out from the presence of the LORD and consumed them, and they died before the LORD" (vv. 1–2).

In this brief sketch, we learn a powerful lesson about worship. There is no question that these two men were worshipers of the true God. The question is, how did they choose to worship?

Many suggest that part of their problem was worshiping God while drunk (v. 9). The prohibition against drinking and entering the Tent of Meeting is the basis for this interpretation. Others believe that the "unauthorized fire" was key to God's displeasure with their worship (v. 1). It was not the censer in which the incense was burned, but the source of the fire inside it that ignited His anger.

To understand the importance of this incident, it might help to back up and review God's instructions for the offering of sacrifices found in Leviticus 9, concluding with these words: "Fire came out from the presence of the LORD and consumed the burnt offering and the fat portions on the altar" (v. 24). The fire that destroyed Nadab and Abihu was a different kind of fire from God's cleansing, purifying fire.

Perhaps the intent of these men was to draw attention to themselves, to compete with God. He sent fire to the altar; they brought a substitute, representing their own work.

God is clear about how we are to come to Him: "'Among those who approach me I will show myself holy; in the sight of all the people I will be honored'" (10:3). Their offering did not respect the holiness of God, nor did it honor Him. Prideful worship draws attention to self. Nadab and Abihu worshiped God, but in a self-styled manner—as did the first king of Israel. . . .

Saul (1 Sam. 13:1–14). It is interesting to note how often God makes His people wait until His purposes are accomplished before He works on their behalf. During the time of the Exodus, when Pharaoh's army was closing in on the people of Israel, God said to them through Moses, "Stand firm and you will see the deliverance the Lord will bring you today" (Ex. 14:13). So they waited while the pillar of cloud moved between them and the advancing enemy. They waited "throughout the night" (v. 20)! The parting of the sea was not a quick miracle, but one that involved standing still and waiting.

Now God is again making His people wait. Seven long days have passed since the prophet Samuel promised to meet King Saul on the battleground to pray for victory. The war with the Philistines is heating up. Some of Saul's troops are in hiding, and others have deserted. The remaining soldiers are described as "quaking with fear" (1 Sam. 13:7).

With the prophet still nowhere in sight and the situation growing more desperate, Saul isn't willing to wait any longer. "Bring me the burnt offering and the fellowship offerings," he says, and proceeds to offer them himself (v. 9). This time it is not a matter of an unauthorized element of worship, but of an "unauthorized" person making the offering.

Just as Saul finished the ceremony, Samuel arrived, and King Saul went out to greet him. "'What have you done?' asked Samuel. Saul replied, 'When I saw that the men were scattering, and that you did not come at the set time, and that the Philistines were assembling at Micmash, I thought, "Now the Philistines will come down against me at Gilgal, and I have not sought the Lord's favor." So I felt compelled to offer the burnt offering'" (vv. 11–12).

Count the number of "I's" in this sentence. "I saw" . . . "I thought" . . . "I have not sought" . . . "I felt compelled." Panicky, impatient, and self-absorbed, Saul "acted foolishly," according to Samuel. He continued, "You have not kept the command the Lord your God gave you; if you had, he would have established your kingdom over Israel for all time. But now your kingdom will not endure; the Lord has sought out a man after his own heart and appointed him leader of his people, because you have not kept the Lord's command" (vv. 13–14).

Tough consequence—the loss of a kingdom as a result of pride and disobedience. Saul believed that he could act on his own without consulting God. Again, it was not a question of *whom* he was worshiping but *how*. In light of his current predicament, the king chose to worship God the way he wanted to.

And then there was . . .

Uzzah (2 Sam. 6:6–7). It must have been a majestic procession. Thirty thousand of David's chosen men had been selected to bring the ark of God to Jerusalem. A new cart had been made for the occasion. The whole house of Israel was celebrating with singing, accompanied by harps, lyres, tambourines, sistrums, and cymbals.

There was a problem though. The ark was not being moved in the way God had instructed. David had consulted the military leaders instead of the priests. He'd planned the event with pomp and pageantry—and irreverence.

"When they came to the threshing floor of Nacon, Uzzah reached out and took hold of the ark of God, because the oxen stumbled. The LORD'S anger burned against Uzzah because of his irreverent act; therefore God struck him down and he died there beside the ark of God" (vv. 6–7). On a day of celebration, an act of worship of the true God came to a sudden, unexpected, dramatic end as God struck dead a worshiper.

God demonstrated by the death of Uzzah the importance of following His clear instructions. Uzzah's intention—to steady the ark—was good. David, too, was sincere in his desire to celebrate the return of the ark to Jerusalem. But sincerity is not the issue. The true God simply cannot be worshiped in a self-styled manner.

Yet throughout the ages, people have misunderstood true worship, have twisted and distorted it, have even rebelled against it in their hearts, all while going through the motions.

The Perversion of Worship (Matt. 15:1–9)

The Jewish people of Jesus' day paid close attention to "the tradition of the elders" (v. 2). These were the rules and regulations stipulated by the rabbis, the interpretations and applications of the law of Moses that governed their daily life. Around A.D. 200 these rules were put into writing in the Mishnah.

Yet some of these traditions were sometimes used to avoid obeying God's commands! One cited by Jesus in these verses was the practice of declaring that particular items, including money, were *korban*, gifts dedicated to God. This practice allowed a greedy son, for example, to bypass doing his duty to his parents. If declared *korban*, the money or goods that could have been used to support them could then be withheld.

Indignant, Jesus quoted the prophet Isaiah: "'These people honor me with their lips, but their hearts are far from me. They worship me in vain; their teachings are but rules taught by men'" (vv. 8–9). These rule-keepers were law-breakers. God was not pleased with their mockery.

So, what is it that delights God's heart? How can we bring worship that honors and exalts Him? If all of these outward acts, prompted by false motives, are unacceptable, what is acceptable worship to the God of the universe?

The Price of True Worship (Heb. 11–12)

Once again the Word of God holds the key to the one who hungers and thirsts for truth. In the eleventh chapter of the Book of Hebrews is a catalog of true worshipers, heroes of the faith, sometimes referred to as the Hall of Fame. Victory after victory, triumph after triumph is recorded here. Men and women who persevered and received God's commendation for lives of faithful service.

It appears, however, as we read on, that many of these heroes paid a great price. "Others were tortured and refused to be released. . . . Some faced jeers and flogging, while still others were chained and put in prison. They were stoned; they were sawed in two; they were put to death by the sword. They went about in sheepskins and goatskins, destitute, persecuted and mistreated—the world was not worthy of them" (11:35–38). What does this list of troubles and persecutions have to do with worship?

From this roll call of heroism, we move into the twelfth chapter of Hebrews, which pictures these who have gone before as "a great cloud of witnesses" (12:1), encouraging us to persevere in our own race to the finish line. "Let us fix our eyes on Jesus, the author and perfecter of our faith, who for the joy set before him endured the cross, scorning its shame, and sat down at the right hand of the throne of God" (v. 2)— the place of intimacy with the Father, *the heart of worship*!

We, too, can arrive at that destination. The chapter continues by reminding us that true worship involves discipline (vv. 7–11) and submission to God's direction (vv. 12–16). But if we are faithful, we will "come to Mount Zion, to the heavenly Jerusalem, the city of the living God. . . . to thousands upon thousands of angels in joyful assembly, to the church of the firstborn, whose names are written in heaven. You [will] come to God, the judge of all men . . . , to Jesus the mediator of a new covenant. . . . Therefore, since we are receiving a kingdom that cannot be shaken, let us be thankful, *and so worship God acceptably with reverence and awe, for our 'God is a consuming fire'*" (vv. 22–24, 28–29).

We are called to worship not as an incidental activity, but as an awesome expectation by God! In the midst of real life— the nitty-gritty, extreme persecution, uncertainty, and even death—we are *expected* to worship.

Making It Real

Determining to "fix your eyes on Jesus" is the beginning point of acceptable worship as a way of life. There is no room in that decision for self, no place for a god of your own choosing, or a different form for God, or worshiping Him any way you please.

When pride elevates self over Scripture, we put ourselves in danger. "Our God is a consuming fire," and He has created us for fellowship with Him and Him alone.

To rid yourself of pride once and for all, try the following:

• Read Hebrews 12:7–11. Read it again. Study the lesson on discipline that Paul presents here. Any "hardship" you may be enduring right now may be considered "discipline" from God. Celebrate! That means that you're His child, "for what son is not disciplined by his father?" (v. 7). And the discipline will produce "a harvest of righteousness and peace for those who have been trained by it" (v. 11).

• Now read Hebrews 12:12–16. These are the steps to the throne of God, including fortifying inner strength, peace, holiness, sexual purity, and getting rid of bitterness. Decide today that you will take another step each day toward authentic worship.

Check your pride. Check it at the door before you worship. Better yet, just check it out of your life for good. Then bring all your offerings before God, asking Him to help you worship acceptably. It's really all that matters.

GOING DEEPER
(A Personal Study Guide)

Part 1—Getting into the Word

Prayer—Pride, one of the greatest hindrances to acceptable worship, can also be one of the greatest hindrances to effective prayer. In developing the heart God desires, pride must be recognized if it is present. Ask God to search your heart and reveal any pockets of pride. Invite Him to uproot them so that nothing hinders your worship.

Reading/Hearing God's Word—Instead of a single book or passage of Scripture, this chapter explores a variety of readings. Choose one. Or, if you are in a small group study, try assigning each member a different selection for review and discussion. Someone else may have a different perspective on something you've read.

Understanding God's Word—Reread your passage. Underline any key phrases or ideas. Then answer the following questions:

1. How did pride enter this worship scene and result in God's judgment?

_____

_____

_____

2. How do these accounts of worship gone wrong reinforce the statement, "In an anything-goes world, some people have a casual attitude toward worship as well"?

_____

_____

_____

Meditating on God's Word—Write a brief summary of a meaningful verse or idea, or paraphrase one of the worship scenes in this chapter.

_____
_____
_____
_____

Part 2—The Word in Review

Introduction

> The pizza story reminds us that we can't "order" worship any way we want it without considering God's preference in the matter. The question is, how does He want us to worship Him?

I. The One We Worship (Ex. 20:3)

II. Our Perception of the One We Worship (Ex. 32:1–8)

III. The Pride that Can Destroy Worship

    A. Nadab and Abihu (Lev. 10:1–3)
    B. Saul (1 Sam. 13:1–14)
    C. Uzzah (2 Sam. 6:6–7)

IV. The Perversion of Worship (Matt. 15:1–9)

V. The Price of True Worship (Heb. 11–12)

Part 3—Taking the Word into My World

Not all worship is acceptable by God's standards. Sometimes He even rejects our lame attempts. Are you beginning to get the message? If so, you are developing the heart of worship God desires.

While we may think that the worship of false gods is not a temptation, the list of enticements includes money. Read again Job 31:24–28. What is the present-day equivalent of these verses?

_____

_____

_____

Exodus 32:1–8 strikes at the heart of the attitude that says, "I worship God as I perceive Him to be." What are some examples of people remaking God into the image they choose? Could misquoted, misinterpreted, misapplied Scripture be part of the problem?

_____

_____

_____

Define *pride* in your own words.

_____

_____

_____

After reading about examples of prideful worship as found in the Bible, think about ways in which pride can manifest itself in our worship today. Is it possible for pride to affect your times of personal worship? In what ways?

_____

_____

_____

Ask yourself, Whom do I worship? Why do I worship? What drives me? Am I guilty of idolatry? What ultimate rewards am I seeking?

_____

_____

_____

_____

_____

Part 4—Grabbing Hold

Typically, the subject of unacceptable worship focuses on a critique of worship style in a church. Style is not the subject of the passages we have studied. The subject is the heart. To grab hold of this lesson is to be willing to ask God to help you examine your heart, seeking to root out pride or any other hindrance to acceptable worship.

Are you also willing to pay the price of true worship, to submit to His discipline and obey His promptings to live a life of holiness? A true worshiper doesn't count the cost but "fixes his eyes on Jesus."

CHAPTER 11

ALL THAT MATTERS

*"Unless there is with us that which is above us,
we shall soon yield to that which is around us."*
— P. T. Forsyth

It would be an understatement to say that the city was crowded. On a typical day, this was the home of perhaps a hundred thousand people, relatively small compared to some of the vast metropolitan areas of our modern world, but of great importance in the first century. When the pilgrims came to observe the annual feast days—by foot, on donkey or camel, or in ox-drawn carts—the city swelled to possibly four times its size, as upwards of a quarter of a million visitors ascended upon Jerusalem. ("Ascended," because one always goes "up to Jerusalem," which is built on hilly terrain.)

Passover season was like a family reunion for an entire nation. The roads teemed with travelers moving in one direction, the noise and confusion punctuated with joyful sounds of praise as the people anticipated the great celebration to come.

We still have their songbook. Psalms 120–134 are all "songs of ascents." Those who were heading to the Holy City would have cried to one another: "I rejoiced with those who said to me, 'Let us go to the house of the LORD.' Our feet are standing in your gates, O Jerusalem. . . . That is where the tribes go up, the tribes of the LORD, to praise the name of the LORD" (Ps. 122:1–2, 4). Yes, the journey may have been hard, but the worship was electrifying.

Among the thousands of joyous worshipers on this Passover Eve was One who had "resolutely set out for

Jerusalem" (Luke 9:51). In obedience to the Word of God, the people gathered for this annual feast, and in obedience to the God of the Word, Jesus joined them for what would be the final Passover, the sacrifice of the One John had called "the Lamb of God."

It all began on that first Palm Sunday with Jesus' unusual request—"Go . . . find a donkey . . . with her colt by her," He told His disciples (Matt. 21:2). By the time He arrived at the Mount of Olives, unparalleled spontaneous praise erupted, a scene so intense that if the people could have been silenced, the stones would have cried out. Pilgrims lined the road from the crest of the hill to the gate of the city. Garments carpeted the path along which the animal trod, carrying Jesus in a regal simplicity reminiscent of Solomon's arrival at Gihon (1 Kings 1). The branches of palm trees became instruments of praise.

What humility. What sacrifice. What love. He, the Creator of the universe, arriving in the Holy City on a lowly beast of burden instead of a king's chariot. Heralded, not with trumpets and fanfare, but with the glad greetings of simple folk. Ready to be crowned, not with gold, but with thorns. This is the path to praise, the way to worship.

If you sincerely desire what God wants, then your heart's journey will be shaped by that longing, that desire to live out and experience the joy of not only the liturgy of worship but the life of worship.

Back to the Bible

The Word of God is invaluable in developing a heart of worship. Where else do we find God's guidelines for living? Who else knows His heart as well as those inspired writers of Holy Scripture?

The first stirring of an interest in worship came through the study of the Word—and a service unlike anything I had experienced previously. But first things first.

I had heard the comments about the lack of true worship in many churches, just as I had heard some bemoan the lack of solid expository preaching. My interest was aroused, and I

148

began studying the subject of worship in the Bible as well as in the writings of contemporary authors. In combination, the effect was like the proverbial light turning on.

Increasingly, I became aware of the frequency with which the word *worship* appears in the Bible. I found examples of true worshipers as well as those whose motives were selfish and impure. Whole worship "scenes" seemed to leap off the pages. I learned what God wants and what He does not want from worshipers.

As baseball legend Yogi Berra once said, "It is amazing how much you can see just by looking." The more I looked, the more I saw! Gideon, worshiping outside that enemy soldier's tent; Peter, worshiping in the fishing boat; Jesus, praying to the Father and offering the ultimate sacrifice on the cross.

In this book it has been my intent to highlight God's Word on worship, not my opinion. Look back over the chapters you have read. Chapter 1 explores Job 1; chapters 2 and 3, Isaiah 1; chapter 4, Isaiah 6; chapter 5, John 4; and so on. It is far more important to consider the Sacred Scriptures' stance on worship than the words of one who is learning to worship.

God did not give us His Word just to increase our knowledge, however, but to affect the way we live. The Bible, written to an agricultural society, is applicable to our information age. It is the eternal Word of God, not limited by time or location, still speaking truth. The only limitation may be in our failure to show how it impacts real life today.

When Worship "Got Real"

Worship moved from past historical fact to present reality in a worship service. I was away from home attending a class while working on my doctorate. Typically a group of us would head out to church on Wednesday night. It was the first of those forays that put me in the midst of a service unlike any I had ever attended. I was well versed in traditional worship forms but unacquainted with the freer expression of faith practiced by some Christians. Rather than a style of service, interrupted by announcing page numbers, waiting for people to turn in the songbooks to the next hymn, long periods of silence while someone from the back row made his way to the platform to sing or pray, this service flowed from song to prayer to testimony to song again with fluid grace. And it was so personal—directed *to* God rather than singing/talking *about* God.

This was a worship event in which there were no performers, only participants. God alone received the glory, interacting with the worshipers as we followed the Spirit's lead. I looked around, with perhaps too much of the student mind-set, observing, analyzing, mentally dissecting. Theology was intersecting with reality and worship was made real for me that night. It was an experience that transcended pure reason alone.

Although I appreciate my intellectuality, I don't mind admitting that I have feelings. Still, services such as the one described may evoke sensations that can be a counterfeit for real worship. We need a safety net. That safety net is the grid of biblical truth.

To decide what we believe on the basis of experience alone is dangerous, potentially lethal. Yet we must understand that the Christian life will be both objective and subjective. As Warren Wiersbe notes, "Worship is not an unexpressed feeling, nor is it an empty formality."[1]

Not only was I learning an objective truth in my study of the Bible, but I was seeing it applied. I needed to see how worship "worked." It was not just a matter of having an experience and calling it "truth," but of seeing truth applied to worship.

My lessons have been ongoing, since worship is not static but ever changing—not in its focus but in its forms. It is as diverse in form as people are diverse. The subjective experiences will vary, but the objective truth must not. Like those mentioned in the Barna survey at the beginning of this book, I had stood wanting what I saw others experiencing in their worship. Now it was happening!

Winning the Worship Wars

There came a point in which my worship pilgrimage went public, a sermonic "IPO" that in its initial offering may not have had the appearance of a blue chip stock, but did show promise. This leads our thinking from personal to corporate application, from what was going on in a pastor's heart to how it affected the congregation.

The more I learned, the more I wanted to share. Out of my experience came a sermon series on worship and an attempt to implement my newfound knowledge in the services of the church I was pastoring at the time. I wanted our people to see what I was seeing. I wanted to shout, "Look at what God is saying to us!" — the true definition of expository preaching.

The beauty of exposition lies in the whole truth that God is revealing to us, not in bits and pieces sewn together like a patchwork quilt. Quilters take scraps of fabric and make a pattern of their own choosing. Some preachers use isolated texts to do the same thing. Expositors stay with a passage, present the central thrust, and develop the main points from the passage. The expositor must still exercise care to be an "exegete" — getting out of the passage what it says and not what he or she wants it to say.

Even when a leader is discreet and sensitive to the needs and preferences of others, change is difficult. You cannot move without producing friction. Worship wars are real, and the battles waged are sometimes bloody, in the figurative sense.

In an attempt to bring our local congregation along in their understanding of worship, I took the following steps:

I taught the Word. There is no better place to begin than the immutable Word of God. I taught small groups, rotating from adult class to adult class, using a series of lessons I had developed. The small group context allowed for interaction. The people could hear my heart, listen to my concerns, and sense that it was not just a matter of preference but biblical truth.

Elements of biblical worship were incorporated into our services. As we studied, we began to develop a mentality that moved away from a view of a worship service in only two parts—preliminaries and preaching. The congregation was no longer regarded as the audience. God was the audience. There was a striving for balance—of content, emotion, and audience awareness.

Special opportunities for instruction were used. Worship scenes from the Bible would occasionally be a part of the text examined that day. Passages highlighting worship were used. These biblical references were needed to help the people understand the significance of worship in the Bible and in the lives of early worshipers. A friend once said, "People are down on what they are not up on." I tried to keep that in mind, explaining, repeating myself, trying a variety of opportunities to teach and model biblical worship.

An additional opportunity was "field trips." On one occasion I took a small group to a worship workshop. Afterwards one of the people commented, "Now I understand what you have been talking about." Seeing, experiencing for themselves, helped them understand.

I didn't do it alone. Instead, we formed a "Worship Ministry Group." They were not called a "committee" because of my disdain for the word. In preparing our worship folder, our church secretary once made a typo. The title of the hymn became, "Come All Christians, Be Committeed." Truer words may never have been mistyped!

This group was composed of a variety of people of varying ages and with varying interests and abilities. Some were long-time members of the congregation; others, newcomers. They entered into the planning of our worship services, helping carry the load, giving input, providing differing perspectives.

Was this all done without ripples? I wish! Sometimes the ripples became waves, some of which felt like tsunamis! Still, if worship is so important to God that He seeks worshipers, it must be important enough for us to study, change, and implement, risking the accompanying disagreement and misunderstanding.

◆

The things that we cling to so tenaciously today may well be what split the church in the past. One example is congregational singing. In Jonathan Edwards's day, churches in New England divided over the issue of everyone singing together in the same key and tempo, and the issue of men and women singing together. So, when the instrumentalist plays the introduction to give you the key and the song leader says, "Let's all sing together," you are engaging in behavior that fueled the worship wars of seventeenth-century New England.

For worship to be a time of contemplation, not contention, try this:

Open your heart to the teaching of the Word. I sometimes say that we hold the Bible in high regard but just under personal opinion. That is not how it is to be. We are to bring ourselves under the Word, allowing it to change us. We need to read the Word, learn the Word, and live the Word.

Grant grace to those who disagree. Grace accepts the beauty in a rainbow of tastes, styles, and preferences. The Bible nowhere teaches one style. Worship trends are not static either. What is done in the church today is not the same as in the first-century church. Nor is worship the same around the world, but varies with location and culture. God's Word teaches that true worship is first a heart issue, then is demonstrated in a variety of postures and practices.

Making It Real

To be a person whose worship is a way of life:

• Consider what prompts you to worship. Can life events remind you of the working of God in your life?

• Seek to understand God, through His Word, so that the revelation of who He is will reveal who you are. Then be willing to live for His purposes, His glory.

• Be careful not to read into worship what you want it to mean. Listen carefully to the instruction of Jesus. Meet with God personally and allow yourself to know Him more intimately.

- Don't be sidetracked by pride or a personal agenda.
- Live all of life in response to God.

What is it that really matters? Worship. Biblical worship. We need to read carefully, learn well, and live out what the Bible teaches, worshiping in spirit and in truth. For when all the sermons have been preached, all the anthems sung, all the worship renewal workshops conducted, and all our innovations come and gone, all that matters is that we can say with our whole being, "Worthy is the Lamb!"

GOING DEEPER
(A Personal Study Guide)

The final chapter of this book is a bit different in that no major Scripture passage is examined. This chapter is more of a testimony than a teaching. It is a conclusion—but only to the writing of the book. For yourself, think of it as a commencement—the beginning of your continued effort to develop the heart of worship that pleases and glorifies God.

Part 1—Getting into the Word

Prayer—As you bring this study to a conclusion, ask God to help you assimilate into your life the lessons learned, and make it your goal to develop as a true worshiper.

Reading/Hearing God's Word—Read or listen to Revelation 4–5. Take time to note the details in this worship scene, which takes place in the throne room of heaven itself.

_____

_____

_____

Understanding God's Word—Read those chapters again. Underline any key phrases or ideas that seem especially meaningful to you. Then answer the following questions:

1. Who are the participants in this worship scene?

_____

_____

2. Who is the object of their worship?

_____

_____

3. Psalm 29:1-2 reminds us to ascribe glory to God. What do these verses say about God?

_____

_____

_____

Meditating on God's Word—Wherever you are right now, without waiting for heaven, you can join the great chorus of twenty-four elders, the living creatures, and the thousands upon thousands of angels who praise God continually, saying:

Holy, holy, holy
is the Lord God Almighty,
who was, and is, and is to come.

You are worthy, our Lord and God,
to receive glory and honor and power,
for you created all things,
and by your will they were created and have their being.
(Rev. 4:8, 11)

True worshipers never grow weary of singing God's praises. They are overwhelmed by His grace and goodness and acknowledge His "worth-ship." Worship comes naturally and effortlessly, welling up out of hearts of gratitude.

Part 2—The Word in Review

Retrace the path this book has taken. A logical progression challenges you to make worship a central part of your life every day, not confining it to a few hours once or twice a week. Following this progression, we moved to the issue of the heart, to suggested biblical methods for changing attitudes toward worship, to implementation of worship principles, and finally, to a commitment to put those principles into action.

Chapter titles provide a comprehensive review:

Chapter 1: Real Life, Real Worship (Job 1)

Chapter 2: Stop the Music (Isaiah 1:1–20)

Chapter 3: When the Band Was Banned (Isaiah 1:10–20)

Chapter 4: The Change Agent (Isaiah 6)

Chapter 5: Well on the Way to Worship (John 4:10–26)

Chapter 6: Worship: A Work in Process (Nehemiah 1)

Chapter 7: The Holy Balance: Heart and Head (Psalm 95, John 4:23–24)

Chapter 8: The Praise of Our Lives (Romans 12:1)

Chapter 9: The Most Important Thing (Nehemiah 12:27–43)

Chapter 10: Unacceptable Worship (Selected Scriptures)

Chapter 11: All That Matters

Part 3—Taking the Word into My World

1. As you reread the list of chapter titles, can you recall the point of each lesson?

Chapter 1: _____

Chapter 2: _____

Chapter 3: _____

Chapter 4: _____

Chapter 5: _____

Chapter 6: _____

Chapter 7: _____

Chapter 8: _____

Chapter 9: _____

Chapter 10: _____

Chapter 11: _____

2. Which chapter(s) were most applicable to your life?

_____

_____

_____

3. What course of action have you taken to apply specific lessons to your life?

_____

_____

_____

Part 4—Grabbing Hold

God wants to have intimate communion with you. You were created for this deep fellowship with the One who knows you best and loves you most.

Write a prayer of commitment, telling Him your intention to be faithful in developing the heart He desires. Include in that prayer specific steps you will take so that worship will become a natural outgrowth of recognizing and appreciating His goodness and grace in all the events of your life—every day.

_____

_____

_____

_____

_____

_____

_____

_____

_____

_____

NOTES

Introduction

1. Barna Research Online, "Worship Tops the List of Important Church-Based Experiences" (http://www.barna.org., February 19, 2001).

2. Jerry Bridges, *I Exalt You, O God* (Colorado Springs, Colo.: Waterbrook Press, 2001), p. 3.

3. Ibid., pp. 2–3.

Chapter 1 — Real Life, Real Worship

1. Philip Yancey, *Disappointment with God* (Grand Rapids, Mich.: Zondervan Publishing House, 1988), p. 162.

Chapter 2 — Stop the Music

1. Barna Research Online, "Worship," February 19, 2001.

Chapter 3 — When the Band Was Banned

1. Mike Pilavachi, "Coming Back to the Heart of Worship," *Worship Together Magazine* (http://www.worshiptogether.com, January 1, 2000.)

2. Ben Patterson, "Why the Sermon?," *Leadership Journal*, Summer 1984.

3. Warren W. Wiersbe, *Real Worship* (Grand Rapids, Mich.: Baker Book House, 2000), p. 26.

Chapter 4 — The Change Agent

1. John Piper, "Preaching As Worship: Meditations on Expository Exultation," *Trinity Journal*, 1995, p. 30.

Chapter 5 — Well on the Way to Worship

1. Piper, *Desiring God* (Portland, Oreg.: Multnomah Press, 1988), p. 61.

2. From the *NIV Study Bible* (Grand Rapids, Mich.: Zondervan Publishing House, 1995), p. 1598.

3. W. E. Vine, *Expository Dictionary of New Testament Words*, 4 vols. (London, Marshall, Morgan & Scott; second Zondervan printing, Grand Rapids, Mich.: Zondervan Publishing House, 1982), p. 236.

4. Wiersbe, *Real Worship*, p. 26.

Chapter 6 — Worship: A Work in Process

1. D. A. Carson, *A Call to Spiritual Reformation* (Grand Rapids, Mich.: Baker Book House, 1992), pp. 28–29.

Chapter 7 — The Holy Balance: Heart and Head

1. Jack Hayford, *Worship His Majesty* (Ventura, Calif.: Regal Books, 2000), p. 150.

2. Wiersbe, *Real Worship*, p. 82.

3. John MacArthur, *The Ultimate Priority* (Chicago: Moody Press, 1983), p. 121.

4. Piper, *Desiring God*, p. 65.

Chapter 8 — The Praise of Our Lives

1. John Stott, *Romans: God's Good News for the World* (Downers Grove, Ill.: InterVarsity Press, 1994), p. 312.

2. Bishop Handley Moule, quoted in Stott, ibid., p. 312.

Chapter 9 — The Most Important Thing

1. Colin Owen, "*The Most Important Thing about Worship,*" Watton on the Web/Christian Resource Centre (http://www.gurney.co.uk/watton/worship/articles).

2. MacArthur, *The Ultimate Priority*, p. 14.

3. J. I. Packer, *A Passion for Faithfulness* (Wheaton, Ill.: Crossway Books, 1995), p. 163.

Chapter 11 — All That Matters

1. Wiersbe, *Real Worship*, p. 21.